SEASONS *of* BLESSING

The Promises and Provision of God's Appointed Times

SEASONS *of* BLESSING
The Promises and Provision
of God's Appointed Times

by David Cerullo

ISBN: 978-1-936177-25-7

Published by:

INSPIRATION MINISTRIES
PO Box 7750
Charlotte, NC 28241

+1 803-578-1899

inspiration.org

Printed in the United States of America.

Don't Miss Your Appointments With God!

*"These are the appointed feasts of the LORD that
you shall proclaim as holy convocations;
they are My appointed feasts."*

– Leviticus 23:2-3 ESV

*"My appointed time is near. I am going to celebrate
the Passover with my disciples."*

– Jesus, Matthew 26:18 NIV

*"Stand at the crossroads and look;
ask for the ancient paths,
ask where the good way is, and walk in it,
and you will find rest for your souls."*

– Jeremiah 6:16 NIV

TABLE OF CONTENTS

GET READY TO BE BLESSED!

Dear Friends,

God is a God of seasons and timing. Yes, your Heavenly Father wants to bless you every day, but His Word describes special *"appointed times"* when He wants to break into the circumstances of your life in extraordinary ways.

Just as God sent His Son in the *"fullness of time"* (Galatians 4:4-5), the feasts of Passover, Pentecost, and Tabernacles are appointed times when He wants to draw close to you...to meet with you and bless you with His promises...and when He invites you to come before Him with your special offerings to honor and worship Him.

Your Heavenly Father loves you and wants to step into the circumstances of your life with His supernatural breakthroughs today! But some of His most amazing spiritual blessings are offered to us through the Biblical feasts He ordained in Exodus 23 and Leviticus 23. These passages describe three *"holy convocations"* or *"appointed times"* — special times on God's calendar when He wants to meet with us and bless our lives in miraculous ways.

The Lord decreed that these three appointed feasts are to be celebrated *perpetually* throughout all generations...yes, FOREVER (Leviticus 23:40-41). These aren't just *Israel's* feasts or the *church's* feasts — they're the *Lord's* feasts!

For example, in referring to the Feast of Passover, the Bible says plainly that it was not a celebration for the Israelites, but *"for the LORD"*:

*It is a night to be **observed for the LORD** for having brought them out from the land of Egypt; **this night is for the LORD**, to be observed by all the sons of Israel **throughout their generations*** (Exodus 12:42 NASB).

Although the Bible mentions seven feasts in all, three of them are given special emphasis: Passover, Pentecost, and Tabernacles (or Booths). God's instructions about these feasts aren't tied to an old or a new covenant. He simply tells us emphatically: *"Three times you **shall** keep a feast to Me in the year"* (Exodus 23:14). This was a direct and insistent command from the Lord!

Passover is celebrated in the springtime, along with the Feast of Unleavened Bread, Feast of Firstfruits, and then — 50 days later — the Feast of Pentecost. The Feast of Tabernacles is in the fall of the year, and this special season of blessing is preceded by ten "Days of Awe" — starting with the Feast of Trumpets *(Rosh Hashanah)* and concluding with the Day of Atonement.

I wrote this book because I've seen supernatural blessings and favor unleashed as my wife Barbara and I have kept these special appointments with God. We've discovered that amazing blessings can be released when we observe the feasts of the Lord…obey His Word… and honor Him by sowing special financial seeds into His Kingdom.

I'm convinced this message will change your life as well. No matter what you may be going through today, God's loving favor will take you from the land of NOT ENOUGH or BARELY ENOUGH to His amazing land of MORE THAN ENOUGH.

God bless you!

David Cerullo

1 Who Stole Your Blessings?

If you had something of great value, and someone stole it, wouldn't you feel angry? I sure would. But in the case of the blessings available through the Lord's *"appointed times,"* most Believers don't even recognize that they've been robbed!

The devil is a thief, intent on stealing God's blessings from your life. Jesus made this clear when He said, *"The thief comes only to steal and kill and destroy; I have come that they may have life, and have it to the full"* (John 10:10 NIV).

Yet the enemy uses people to do his work, and sometimes he even uses people who are well-meaning, but deceived. I believe this was the case when the Roman Emperor Constantine mixed Christianity with pagan practices in an effort to get the pagans to convert to Christianity. This tragic development in 325 AD resulted in a superficial brand of Christianity that incorporated pagan rituals into the church and forced Believers to abandon their Jewish roots and mindset.

Despite facing horrific persecution, the church had been blessed with God's prosperity and power. Constantine promised that if God's people would forsake the Biblical principles and Hebraic mindset that had led to their incredible blessings, the persecution would stop.

The Christians were about to be robbed of something very precious, and they didn't even realize what was happening to them.

So the church gained peace, but lost its true identity. By forsaking its Hebraic roots, the church forfeited the spiritual power it once enjoyed. And with its spiritual power gone, the church lost much of the prosperity and favor it once enjoyed.

The compromise initiated by Constantine is *still* holding many Christians in bondage and financial lack today. The only way to unlock God's storehouse of blessing, favor, and prosperity is to get back into alignment with His original plan. We must return to *"the ancient paths,"* as God warned through the prophet Jeremiah:

> *My people have forgotten Me, they have burned incense to worthless idols. And they have caused themselves to stumble in their ways, from the ancient paths, to walk in pathways and not on a highway* (Jeremiah 18:15).

What are the *"ancient paths"* God was speaking about here? Why did He feel it necessary to warn His people? And how do the Lord's prescribed feasts pertain to the ancient blessings He wants us to walk in?

This is such an important matter. When Christians fail to tap into God's abundant blessings, His work on earth is hindered. Believers end up lacking the resources needed to carry out our mission to reach the world with the Gospel.

My wife Barbara and I know what it's like to be BROKE, and we also know what it's like to be BLESSED. At one point years ago, I was without a job. We literally had nothing—no money in the bank and none in our pockets. We didn't know how we were going to make our mortgage or car payments, nor did we even have money to buy groceries to feed our family.

One day we had to break open our son Ben's piggy bank just to have money to go to McDonald's for dinner. That was a stressful period, to be sure.

But through it all, Barbara and I kept trusting God and applying His principles in our lives—the same principles I will be sharing with you in this book. Sometimes it was scary, but He met our every need. Now we can testify that the Lord brought us from the land of NOT ENOUGH to the land of MORE THAN ENOUGH!

I'm convinced God wants to do the same for you, my friend. But right now I want you to be honest with yourself. If you aren't experiencing God's blessings and favor today, could it be that you are missing some important ingredient in His recipe to prosper you? Perhaps quite unintentionally, could you be neglecting some vital step His Word commands you to take?

The Bible describes three different yearly cycles marked by what it calls *"the feasts of the Lord"* or God's *"appointed times."* These are the feasts of Passover, Pentecost, and Tabernacles—special days on God's calendar when He wants to bless you in extraordinary ways.

Perhaps you've never even heard of these feasts. Or maybe you've heard of them but never realized they could transform your life and the lives of your loved ones.

Put simply, you've been ROBBED! But in the pages that follow, I'm going to share God's amazing plan to bless you. When you implement this powerful message, I'm confident you can take back EVERYTHING the enemy has stolen from you!

GOD'S SIGNS AND SEASONS 2

Long before God told His people Israel to celebrate special feast days, He laid a foundation in creation. He gave us the sun and moon as celestial timepieces to announce His *"signs and seasons"*:

> *"**Let there be lights** in the firmament of the heavens to divide the day from the night; and let them be for **signs and seasons,** and for **days and years;** and let them be for lights in the firmament of the heavens to give light on the earth"; and it was so. Then God made **two great lights:** the greater light to rule the day, and the lesser light to rule the night. He made the stars also. God set them in the firmament of the heavens to give light on the earth, and to rule over the day and over the night, and to divide the light from the darkness. **And God saw that it was good"***
> (Genesis 1:14-18).

Right from the beginning, God instituted special days and seasons as part of His divine plan for humanity. Long before He gave Moses the Law on Mount Sinai, He said in the literal translation of Genesis 1:14 that He set the moon and sun in the sky as *"banners, signposts, and indicators of His appointed times."*

This means God didn't just put the sun and moon in their place to give us light by day and night. He also put them there as *signs of His*

appointed times and seasons. He gave everything a "rhythm" of days, seasons, and years. Annual cycles were set in place, and the Lord was preparing humanity to fit into the flow and rhythm of those cycles.

From the very first chapter in the Bible, you can see God establishing special seasons and days, weaving this principle into the very fabric of His creation. Why? Because God is a God of plans, designs, order, and structure. Your Heavenly Father has put His loving fingerprints on every aspect of creation, and He wants you to flow in His prescribed rhythm of special favor and breakthroughs.

Just as a wise farmer understands that he must sow his seeds at the optimal time and season, so too God instructs us that there are optimal times when our seeds sown into His Kingdom will reap *extraordinary* harvests.

As we study the feasts of the Lord, keep in mind this foundational principle of *"signs and seasons."* One of the reasons God instituted His *"appointed times"* is to help you synchronize your life with His plans to bless and prosper you.

This principle is illustrated and affirmed throughout the Scriptures. The Lord wants us to be in step with His calendar and the special seasons He has established to bless us. That's why Solomon wrote: *"To everything there is a season, a time for every purpose under heaven"* (Ecclesiastes 3:1). For example, there's *"a right time to plant and another to reap"* (v. 2 MSG).

Make no mistake about it: Synchronizing your life to God's times and seasons is a vital key for unlocking His blessings. And the Lord gave you the annual feasts as a powerful tool for doing exactly that.

Yet one of the confusing things about the Lord's feasts is that He goes by a different calendar than we do. The Hebrew calendar was set to the phases of the moon, and Psalm 104:19 tells us, *"He appointed*

the moon for seasons." However, this often results in quite different outcomes than we see under our current Gregorian calendar, used in Western nations since 1582 AD. One of the main differences is that the Gregorian calendar is set to coincide with cycles of the sun rather than the moon.

Here's a helpful chart to show you the differences between months on the Jewish calendar and the equivalent time period on the Gregorian calendar:

Jewish Calendar	Gregorian Equivalent
Nisan	March – April
Iyar	April – May
Sivan	May – June
Tammuz	June – July
Av	July – August
Elul	August – September
Tishri	September – October
Heshvan	October – November
Kislev	November – December
Tevet	December – January
Shevat	January – February
Adar	February – March

My friend, my point here is not to bore you with intricate details about times and seasons. But you need to understand that our eternal God, who transcends time and space, *has established a calendar.* On that calendar, He has circled special days and seasons when He wants to meet with you and bless you in extraordinary ways.

Look at it this way...

If God spoke to you in an audible voice and told you to meet Him at a certain time and place in order to receive special breakthroughs in your life, would you pay attention? Would you make sure to be there, so you could receive what the Lord wants to give you? I know I would!

Well, you don't really *need* an audible voice on this, do you? God has already set special appointments for you on His calendar. How could anything be more exciting than that?

SEEDTIME AND HARVEST

3

As we'll soon see, each of the Lord's feasts was connected to the Israelites' agrarian economy in some way. This means the principle of *seedtime and harvest* was woven into the very fabric of these special days.

Deuteronomy 16:16 provides an important aspect of God's instructions about how His people should approach Him to celebrate the feasts of Passover, Pentecost, and Tabernacles: *"None shall appear before the Lord **empty-handed.**"*

In other words, in order to be blessed in uncommon ways during these feasts, God's people were told they must bring an *uncommon offering.* This was to be in *addition* to the regular tithes and offerings that were part of their worship and devotion to the Lord.

It really shouldn't surprise us that the principle of seedtime and harvest would be part of God's plan to bless His people during the feasts. The creation account in Genesis 1 describes how foundational this is for a life of abundance and fruitfulness:

> *Then God said, "Let the earth bring forth grass, the herb that yields **seed**, and the fruit tree that **yields fruit** according to its kind, whose **seed** is in itself, on the earth"; and it was so. And*

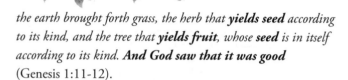

*the earth brought forth grass, the herb that **yields seed** according to its kind, and the tree that **yields fruit**, whose **seed** is in itself according to its kind. **And God saw that it was good*** (Genesis 1:11-12).

In case you had any doubt, this passage makes certain things absolutely clear about the Lord's plan:

- God designed you, and all of His creation, to be FRUITFUL, blessed in every way.

- This fruitfulness is not a matter of random chance, but is produced on the basis of SEEDS.

- God sees this process of seedtime and harvest and says it is GOOD.

No wonder the Lord doesn't want you to come before Him empty-handed. In order to receive an abundant, supernatural harvest, you must first bring Him some *seeds* to multiply!

I frankly get irritated when I hear people say that the laws of seedtime and harvest are obsolete, or that the feasts of the Lord are no longer relevant for Believers today.

Genesis 8:22 tells us plainly:

> *While the earth remains,*
> *Seedtime and harvest,*
> *Cold and heat,*
> *Winter and summer,*
> *And day and night*
> *Shall not cease.*

God says the principles I'm about to share with you *"shall not cease"* as long as the earth remains! While seedtime and harvest is a powerful law all year long, it is supercharged during the Lord's *"appointed times."*

The Lord is ready to bless you with supernatural breakthroughs, as He describes in 2 Chronicles 16:9 TLB: *"The eyes of the Lord search back and forth across the whole earth, looking for people whose hearts are perfect toward him, so that he can show his great power in helping them."*

My friend, God wants to show you His great power today. Whether you need a breakthrough in your health, finances, emotions, or relationships, He is standing ready to come to your aid. But it's crucial to follow *His instructions* in order to see your blessings released.

4 CONDITIONAL PROMISES

Your Heavenly Father loves you more than you can possibly fathom. Just as any good earthly parent, your Father in Heaven wants to bless His children with abundant blessings and a great life—both now and in eternity.

Friend, this can be a day of supernatural breakthroughs for you as you claim God's promises and obey His Word. But you need to understand a critical point about the Lord's promises: Even though He loves you *unconditionally,* His promises and blessings are tied to your actions. Throughout the Scriptures, you'll find God saying, "*I'll* do this…IF *you'll* do that."

Many Believers seem unaware that God's promises are conditional. They can't understand why their prayers aren't answered and their needs go unmet. And sometimes they even conclude that God simply isn't faithful to His Word.

How tragic. Their faith in God's promises is undermined, just because they've neglected to fulfill the conditions He has set.

Don't miss this point: Our faith and obedience are crucial keys to releasing God's blessings, provision, and miracles in our lives. He gives us the keys, but it's up to us to use them!

God ordained the Biblical feasts in Exodus 23 and Leviticus 23 as special *"appointed times"* to meet with Him and receive His blessings. When you observe these seasons on His calendar, He promises to meet with you and bless your life in miraculous ways.

Pause for a moment and ask yourself: If you could ask God for any supernatural turnaround today, what would it be? Do you need a breakthrough in your health? Your finances? Your emotions? Your family? Through the principles I'm going to unveil in this book, your breakthrough can be closer than you think!

God clearly instructed His children that Passover, Pentecost, and Tabernacles (or Booths) are to be *perpetual* feasts, for *all* generations (Leviticus 23:40-41). Yes, there is a BLESSING in store when you commemorate the perpetual feasts, celebrations, and holy convocations God designated as His appointed times.

God *promises* in Exodus 23 and Leviticus 23 that if you bring your offerings and obey what He's told you to do, He will pour out seven specific covenant promises in your life:

1. An angel of God will be assigned to protect you and lead you to your miracles.

2. God will be an enemy to your enemies.

3. The Lord will prosper you.

4. God will take sickness away from you.

5. You will not die before your appointed time.

6. Increase and an inheritance will be yours.

7. What the enemy has stolen will be returned to you.

Take a few minutes to read this list of blessings again, applying them to your own life. Are you going through a spiritual battle that you need

the Lord to fight for you? Are you dealing with a sickness you need Him to heal? Has the devil stolen something you are praying for God to win back for you?

These blessings — *and many more* — are available as you unlock God's supernatural favor during His appointed times.

GOD'S PROPHETIC REHEARSALS 5

God describes Passover, Pentecost, and Tabernacles as *"holy convocations."* The Hebrew word translated as *"convocation"* literally means a "rehearsal." A rehearsal can either be a time to "re-hear" what has been taught or a "practice session" for a later event. It's significant that Passover, Pentecost, and Tabernacles each are a rehearsal of a future prophetic event. Taken together, the Lord's feasts reveal His entire prophetic plan for the ages, from redemption to the establishment of His eternal kingdom.

PASSOVER *(Pesach)* – This feast commemorates God's protection and provision through the blood of the lamb that was sprinkled on the doorposts of the Israelites' homes (Exodus 12). This blood protected them from the death angel that struck the Egyptians.

For Jewish and Christian Believers, Passover is also the celebration of Jesus the Messiah, our perfect Passover Lamb (1 Corinthians 5:8). Passover was a rehearsal of the coming day when Jesus, our Passover Lamb, would lay down His life on the cross and exclaim, *"It is finished!"* (John 19:30)

Right at the beginning of Jesus' ministry, we read the stirring words of John the Baptist when he saw Jesus coming to be baptized by him

in the Jordan River: *"Behold! The Lamb of God who takes away the sin of the world!"* (John 1:29). God's perfect Passover Lamb had finally arrived on the scene, ready to bring deliverance, forgiveness, and healing of humanity's sin and shame.

Passover is celebrated in the first month of the Jewish calendar and during March/April on our Gregorian calendar.

PENTECOST *(Shavuot)* – This feast originally celebrated the first fruits of the harvest. It also commemorated the giving of the Law by God to Moses atop Mount Sinai. The Feast of Pentecost was a rehearsal for the coming day when the Holy Spirit would be poured out on Believers during this feast 50 days after Jesus' Resurrection (Acts 2:1).

Pentecost is a wonderful reminder that we need the power of God in our lives in order to accomplish His will and fulfill our destiny as believers. Jesus described the coming of the Holy Spirit as being endued with *"power from on high"* (Luke 24:49). Through this amazing supernatural power, we're enabled to be Jesus' witnesses throughout the earth (Acts 1:8).

The Greek word for "power" is *dynamis,* from which we get English words such as dynamic or dynamite. It basically means that explosive, miracle-working power is available to us through the Spirit poured out at Pentecost.

At the end of His earthly ministry, Jesus told His disciples about many blessings that would be associated with the work of the Holy Spirit in their lives. In various translations of John 14:26, the Spirit is described as the Helper, Comforter, Companion, Counselor, Intercessor, Advocate, Strengthener, Friend, and the One who is constantly with us in our journey through life.

Aren't you grateful that God offers you the blessings of the Holy

Spirit through the Feast of Pentecost? This powerful prophetic feast is observed in the third month of the Jewish calendar and during May/June on our calendar.

TABERNACLES *(Sukkot)* – God commanded that this feast be observed as a reminder of His care, covering, and protection while the Israelites journeyed from Egypt to the Promised Land. Also known as the "Feast of Booths," this was a time of "double portion" blessings for the people of God.

Tabernacles provides a fantastic opportunity to rejoice in the Lord's goodness and celebrate His blessings. It's a time to remember the seeds we've sown into God's Kingdom and express our profound gratitude for the harvests He has given us in response.

Although the Bible isn't clear about what future event this feast is a rehearsal for, something so significant will happen on planet earth that God says He will command all the nations of the earth to celebrate the Feast of Tabernacles during Jesus' coming reign on earth (Zechariah 14:16). There's also reason to believe that Jesus will return sometime during this prophetic season of the year.

Tabernacles is celebrated in the seventh month of the Jewish calendar (Tishri) and during September/October on our calendar.

God designed these three feasts to be celebrated annually, without fail. They enabled the Israelites to participate in the rhythm of His supernatural abundance — and these same blessings are available to *you* today!

6 PERPETUAL OBSERVANCE, PERPETUAL BLESSINGS

Jesus celebrated the feasts of Passover, Pentecost, and Tabernacles. The disciples celebrated the feasts. The apostle Paul and other leaders celebrated the feasts. The early church celebrated the feasts. So it's misguided to think these feasts are irrelevant to Christians today.

God couldn't have been more clear when he said in Leviticus 23:21 that each of these feasts *"is a holy convocation to you...It shall be a statute* **FOREVER** *in all your dwellings* **throughout your generations.***"*

Right about now, I can hear many Believers object, "But God was speaking in this passage to the Jews in the Old Testament. How does this apply to us as Believers today?"

Do you remember Paul's words in Galatians 3:7-9?

> *Know that only those who are of faith are sons of Abraham. And the Scripture, foreseeing that God would justify the Gentiles by faith, preached the gospel to Abraham beforehand, saying, "In you all the nations shall be blessed." So then those who are of faith are blessed with believing Abraham.*

If you are a Believer in Jesus Christ today, you are a spiritual son or daughter of Abraham. And this means ALL the promises, blessings, and covenants God made with and through Abraham belong to *you*

today! However, in order to experience the blessings given to Abraham, you must *believe* and *obey* the Lord's instructions, as he did.

When God later told the Israelites to celebrate His appointed times *"forever"* and *"throughout your generations,"* He meant exactly that. In fact, Jesus even told His disciples they would be celebrating the Passover meal together after He returned to establish His Kingdom (Matthew 26:29).

But let me be clear: Celebrating these appointed times has *NOTHING* to do with your salvation. You are saved by GRACE and through FAITH (Ephesians 2:8-9), thanks to the blood shed for you by Jesus on the cross.

There's absolutely *nothing* you or I can DO in order to be saved, other than accept God's free gift of salvation (Romans 6:23). You are saved solely on the merit of what Jesus Christ has already DONE for you through His sacrifice on the cross.

But even though it's not an issue of your salvation, observing the Lord's feasts has a *lot* to do with releasing His covenant blessings in your life. Each one of us needs God's supernatural…

- Guidance

- Healing

- Protection

- Provision

- Victory

- Restoration of everything the enemy has stolen from us

And these are just a *few* of the covenant promises God made to His children in Exodus 23 and Leviticus 23…*IF* they would obey Him in all He asked.

Think about it. Israel never had a big army compared to the armies of their enemies. But they weren't depending on the size of their army—they were depending on the size of their GOD and His PROMISES to deliver them!

God was faithful to His Word. He supernaturally provided for them in the wilderness. He gave them food and water, and even kept their shoes from wearing out. Israel lived under a canopy of the Lord's covenant promise to give them supernatural abundance and blessings.

God's Cycle of Blessings

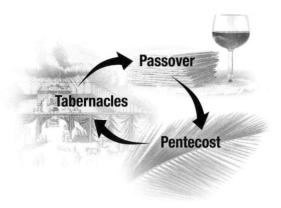

The celebration of these three feasts represents a *cycle* of giving and receiving between God and His people…a *cycle* of seedtime and harvest. From Passover to Pentecost…from Pentecost to Tabernacles… from Tabernacles back to Passover—the Israelites obeyed the Lord and experienced a wonderful rhythm of His supernatural blessings.

As God's people were obedient to bring their special offerings to Him during each feast, the Lord fulfilled His covenant promises listed in Scripture until the next feast time—when they once again brought their special offerings to God, and He once again blessed them for another season.

The Israelites KNEW that if they obeyed the Lord…kept His commandments…and came before Him during these rehearsals with a special offering, they could depend on Him to keep His promises to bless them in extraordinary ways.

There was something very special about the offering God command-ed them to bring during these feasts. He said it was to be in *addition* to their tithes, pledges, and vows (Leviticus 23:37-38). In fact, in the original Hebrew text, God commands them to do something very unusual. He tells them to bring Him the "unholy" offering. *Unholy…* Lord, how can that be?

You see, the tithe already belongs to God. It's not yours, but His. He calls the tithe *"holy to the Lord"* (Leviticus 27:3). In contrast, when God says to bring Him the *unholy*, He means you shouldn't bring Him what already belongs to Him. He wants you to bring Him what belongs to YOU!

So if you need a breakthrough from God, ask yourself: Have you been obedient to Him? Have you been faithful to bring Him your tithes and offerings? Have you been careful to observe His feasts…His rehearsals…His holy convocations? Have you brought Him the special offerings He asked for during these *"appointed times"*?

7 DON'T COME EMPTY-HANDED

Appointments are an incredibly important part of everyday life. You periodically have appointments with your friends…boss…doctor… dentist…car mechanic — and probably many other appointments as well. It's important not to miss an appointment once it has been set.

My friend, just as you need to be faithful to keep these earthly appointments, shouldn't you be much MORE faithful to keep your appointments with your Heavenly Father? Yet people miss appointments all too often, whether out of ignorance or simple disobedience.

Make sure that you don't miss your appointments with God! Whether you need a breakthrough in your health, finances, emotions, or relationships, He has set appointed times to come to your aid — *if* you obey Him.

Referring to these three feasts, Deuteronomy 16:16 says, *"None shall appear before the Lord **empty-handed**."* Yes, God put *conditions* on the promises He made to us, and one of these conditions was to bring Him a special offering during Passover, Pentecost, and Tabernacles.

I'm convinced that many Christians are being robbed of God's intended blessings because they don't think the Old Testament promises apply to them anymore. This is a tragic misunderstanding of Scripture.

God *still* promises that if you obey Him, He will protect you, guide you, provide for you, heal you, and keep you. There are supernatural blessings in store when you celebrate the perpetual feasts, holy convocations, and rehearsals God has designated as His appointed times.

By faith in Jesus Christ, YOU are entitled to claim ALL the covenant promises the Lord made to His covenant people Israel. As we read earlier, Galatians 3:9 says *all* God's promises to Abraham are *yours!*

If you'll take a step of faith and obedience...*if* you'll come before God to honor Him with your worship...*if* you'll prepare Him a special offering...*then* your amazing season of miracles and blessings, breakthroughs and favor, can be at hand. God has made appointments to meet with you...to speak to you...and to bless you. When you obey Him, you can enter into a new dimension of covenant living!

Remember: These aren't just *Israel's* feasts or the *church's* feasts — they're the *Lord's* feasts! His instructions about the feasts aren't tied to an old or a new covenant. He simply tells us emphatically: *"Three times you **shall** keep a **feast to Me** in the year"* (Exodus 23:14).

Notice God's statement that these feasts were to be kept *"to ME."* When you observe the feasts, you are honoring and pleasing *Him.* You are expressing your gratitude for His faithful protection and provision. And through your obedience, you're demonstrating that you are trusting in His promises.

So are you ready to unleash more of God's favor in your life? Then don't miss your appointments to meet with Him and honor Him with your special offerings. He doesn't want you to come to Him empty-handed!

8 REMEMBER THE SKITTLES PRINCIPLE

Sometimes people are surprised to hear that God wants them to bring Him a special offering during His appointed times. "What could that possibly have to do with receiving more of the Lord's blessings?" they ask me.

You'll be able to understand God's perspective better when I share a modern-day story about a man who took his young daughter to her first baseball game. Although she wasn't particularly interested in the game, she *loved* Skittles and was thrilled when a vendor approached their aisle.

The father gladly bought her some Skittles and then asked if she would share some with him. However, the little girl refused, saying firmly, "No, Daddy, they're MINE!"

The girl's dad had purchased the Skittles in the first place, but now she claimed exclusive ownership over them. The father wasn't asking for much, but he expected his daughter to honor their relationship and acknowledge that he was the source of everything she had.

How sad that many of us Believers act in the same way toward our Heavenly Father. It pains them to give tithes and special offerings, even though they would have *nothing at all* without God's blessing. He's the source of *everything* any of us have.

Before we move on to the next chapter, I encourage you to take a few minutes and do this important exercise:

- *First, look at your hands and clench them, making two fists.* This is the posture of those of us who hoard our blessings. However, there's a problem with this picture: If your hands are clenched to hold on to what you have, you won't be in a position to receive anything more. Even worse, you're likely to squash the things you hang on to if you squeeze them too tightly.

- *Now, unclench your fists, and hold your hands with palms facing upward.* You're no longer hanging on to anything, which may make you feel insecure or vulnerable at first. But realize this: When you open up your hands and release all you have to God, your hands are now in a position to receive back from Him an abundance of blessings — MORE THAN ENOUGH!

God wants to bless you abundantly, my friend, but you need to follow His instructions. King Solomon wisely observed:

One person gives freely, yet gains even more;
another withholds unduly, but comes to poverty.
A generous person will prosper;
whoever refreshes others will be refreshed
(Proverbs 11:24-25 NIV).

Do you see how profound this principle is? Your financial breakthroughs aren't released until you trust God and are generous with the resources He's already given you. When you allow fear or unbelief to make you stingy with your resources, the inevitable result will be poverty and financial lack.

However, you've probably met some Christians who say, "I never ask

God to bless me. That would be *selfish!*" But consider this, my friend: It's even MORE selfish for God's people to remain in poverty and financial lack, because then we'll have nothing to give to others.

And perhaps you've always thought you had to twist God's arm in order to receive His blessings. Quite the contrary: He's *eager* to bless you — not just financially, but also in your health, relationships, and peace of mind. He knows that the more you prosper, the more the people around you will observe His blessings and recognize what a great Heavenly Father He is.

Like any father, God wants to be proud of His kids. If your son or daughter was a championship athlete, you would proudly tell your friends, "That's my kid!" In the same way, God wants you to live such victorious lives that the world will take notice of what He has done in your life.

There's a great scene in the movie "Butch Cassidy and the Sundance Kid" where the townspeople ask about Butch and Sundance, "Who *are* those guys?!" These two men stood out from the crowd, and the surrounding bystanders couldn't help but take note.

The world should be asking a similar question when they see you and me: "Who *are* those guys? How do I sign up to receive what they have?"

So even if you've never thought of Biblical prosperity as something you should care about, remember Butch and Sundance. The world is watching. God wants to bless you in extraordinary ways, so you can make an extraordinary impact for His Kingdom.

CRY OUT TO THE LORD

9

Are you in need of a breakthrough in some area of your life today? If you are, you're certainly not alone. At one point or another, every one of us will need a miracle from God — a divine, supernatural intervention — in our health, finances, relationships, or emotions. No one is exempt.

For 430 years, the children of Israel had served as slaves in Egypt. Instead of getting better and better, their plight only grew worse with time. Perhaps you can relate if there's an area of your life where you feel "stuck" in difficult circumstances or oppressed by the enemy.

A turning point came when the Israelites finally cried out to God to end their oppression:

> **The Israelites groaned** in their slavery and **cried out,** and their cry for help because of their slavery went up to God. **God heard their groaning** and he remembered his **covenant** with Abraham, with Isaac and with Jacob. So God looked on the Israelites and was **concerned** about them (Exodus 2:23-25 NIV).

Just as the Lord was concerned about the children of Israel, He is concerned about YOUR situation today as well. Whatever you may be going through, He wants you to *cry out to Him* and remind Him of His covenant with you as a Believer.

In Exodus 6, we see the Lord setting things in motion to release the Israelites from their captivity. He appeared to Moses and said, *"I am the LORD. I appeared to Abraham, to Isaac, and to Jacob, as God Almighty, but by My name LORD I was not known to them. I have also established My covenant with them, to give them the land of Canaan, the land of their pilgrimage, in which they were strangers"* (v. 2).

God reminded Moses of the covenant He had made with Abraham, Isaac, and Jacob — not only to bless them, but also *make them a blessing* throughout the earth (Genesis 12:1-3). This is still God's intention for His people today!

The Lord then assured Moses that He has heard the groaning of the Israelites and seen their bondage. He told Moses to make some audacious promises to these people who had been held in bondage for over four centuries:

> *I am the LORD; I will bring you out from under the burdens of the Egyptians, I will rescue you from their bondage, and I will redeem you with an outstretched arm and with great judgments. I will take you as My people, and I will be your God. Then you shall know that I am the LORD your God who brings you out from under the burdens of the Egyptians. And I will bring you into the land which I swore to give to Abraham, Isaac, and Jacob; and I will give it to you as a heritage: I am the LORD* (vs. 6-8).

Notice that God made five distinct promises to Israel in this passage:

1. *"I will bring you out from under the burdens of the Egyptians."*
2. *"I will rescue you from their bondage."*
3. *"I will redeem you with an outstretched arm and with great judgments."*
4. *"I will take you as My people, and I will be your God."*

5. *"I will bring you into the land which I swore to give to Abraham, Isaac, and Jacob."*

Each of these promises is filled with rich meaning for your life today, but I especially want to call your attention to the contrast between the first promise and the last one. God needed to bring the Israelites OUT of their burdens and bondage in order to bring them INTO the Promised Land of blessings and abundance.

Take a few moments right now to pause and ask the Lord to search your heart. What are the things in your life that He wants to bring you OUT of — things that are hindering you from your destiny and calling? And what kinds of blessings has He promised to bring you INTO as your Promised Land?

God was getting ready to do something amazing for Moses and the children of Israel. He was about to fulfill these five promises, and the Feast of Passover was the beginning of the promised turnaround.

It must have been incredibly difficult for these slaves in Egypt to comprehend that God was preparing them for a new beginning based on His covenant to their forefathers. Not only would He set them free from their bondage, but He would fulfill His promise originally made to Abraham: *"All peoples on earth will be blessed through you"* (Genesis 12:3).

10 GET READY FOR A NEW BEGINNING

Everyone needs a new beginning at one time or another in their life. This may be a new beginning in your health or your finances, your emotions or your relationships. And sometimes you might even need a new beginning in your relationship with God.

If you find yourself needing a turnaround or new beginning in some area of your life today, the feasts of the Lord provide you with wonderful *"appointed times"* for the fresh start you need. In the Gregorian calendar used in the world today, January 1 is New Year's Day, but the Hebrew calendar in the Bible actually includes not just one, but *two,* annual days set aside for new beginnings. What a powerful statement of the Lord's desire to give us breakthroughs and turnarounds!

The first period of new beginnings is the Feast of Passover. When the first Passover was instituted by the Lord, He told Moses and Aaron, *"This month shall be your beginning of months; it shall be the first month of the year to you"* (Exodus 12:1-2). Notice that when God spoke these words, the Israelites were still living as slaves in the land of Egypt. They clearly needed a new beginning — and perhaps you do as well.

During the first Passover feast, the blood of the lamb was sprinkled on the doorposts of the Israelites' homes, and this blood protected them from the death angel that struck the Egyptians. God gave His

people a powerful promise, which still holds powerful meaning for us today:

> *I will pass through the land of Egypt on that night, and will strike all the firstborn in the land of Egypt, both man and beast; and against all the gods of Egypt I will execute judgment: I am the LORD. Now the blood shall be a sign for you on the houses where you are. And when I see the blood, I will pass over you; and the plague shall not be on you to destroy you when I strike the land of Egypt* (vs. 12-13).

On the one hand, the Lord said He was executing judgment against the Egyptians and their gods. But on the other hand, the Passover was a time of His great mercy and grace for those protected by the blood of the unblemished lamb.

Do you see how this beautifully foreshadows what Jesus did for us on the cross? As God's spotless Passover lamb, He shed His blood to purchase our salvation, protection, and favor. Yet the cross was also a picture of God's fierce judgment of sin. As Passover struck a devastating blow to the false gods of the Egyptians, the cross forever crippled Satan's evil kingdom: *"Having disarmed principalities and powers, He made a public spectacle of them, triumphing over them in it"* (Colossians 2:14-15).

Too often, I hear people refer to God's appointed times as "the feasts of Israel" or "Jewish feast days." However, Exodus 12:11 clearly states, *"It is the **LORD's** Passover."* Yes, Passover and the other feasts were given FOR God's people—including us today—but He says these are HIS feasts.

It also grieves the heart of God when people imply that these feasts are no longer relevant for Believers to observe today. He addressed this plainly when Passover was first instituted: *"This day [Passover] shall be to you a memorial; and you shall keep it as a feast to the LORD throughout your generations. You shall keep it as a feast by an everlasting ordinance"* (Exodus 12:14).

My friend, look at this verse again. The feasts of Passover, Pentecost, and Tabernacles are memorials for YOU! God said you should observe these feast days *"throughout your generations"* and as *"an everlasting ordinance."*

So, do you need a new beginning? Then I encourage you to honor the Lord in celebrating His appointed times. Just as the Israelites were set free from their slavery during the first Passover, God wants to set you free today from anything that is hindering you from enjoying His favor and His abundant blessings.

And if it wasn't enough that the Lord instituted Passover as a time of new beginnings, in the fall He provides us with *another* season of new beginnings. The Feast of Tabernacles is preceded by the Feast of Trumpets or *Rosh Hashanah,* which means "Head of the Year." This is the traditional "New Year's Day" on the *civil* calendar of the Jewish people, while Passover is the *spiritual* beginning of a new year.

Think of it: your Heavenly Father is so intent on blessing you and giving you new beginnings that He has provided you with multiple times during the year to receive a fresh start!

YOUR UNBLEMISHED LAMB 11

The first Feast of Passover was the beginning of the Israelites' deliverance from bondage in Egypt. It's also a picture of our deliverance from sin and death by Jesus' death and resurrection, making us new creatures in Him (2 Corinthians 5:17).

At Passover, each family was instructed to sacrifice an unblemished lamb (Exodus 12:3-6). This is a powerful foreshadowing of Jesus, *"the Lamb of God who takes away the sin of the world"* (John 1:29). He was the perfect sacrifice for us on the Cross, because He was *"unblemished and spotless"* (1 Peter 1:18-19) and *"without sin"* (Hebrews 4:15).

But this requirement of an unblemished Passover lamb also speaks of another crucial issue:

You must give God your best!

Despite His clear instructions, the temple priests at one point were dishonoring God by sacrificing blemished and sickly animals:

> *"If I am a master, where is My respect?" says the LORD of hosts to you, O priests who despise My name. But you say, "How have we despised Your name?"*
>
> *"You are presenting defiled food upon My altar...When you present the blind for sacrifice, is it not evil? And when you present*

the lame and sick, is it not evil? Why not offer it to your governor? Would he be pleased with you? Or would he receive you kindly?" says the LORD of hosts...

"I am not pleased with you," says the LORD of hosts, "nor will I accept an offering from you...You bring what was taken by robbery and what is lame or sick...Should I receive that from your hand?" says the LORD (Malachi 1:6-14 NASB).

Do you see how grieved God is when you offer Him less than your best? Rather than giving God unblemished sacrifices, the Israelites were presenting lambs that were blind, lame, or sick. Instead of sacrificing the best of their flocks, they were giving the Lord their surplus and their rejects!

As you celebrate the feasts of Passover, Pentecost, and Tabernacles, you have an excellent opportunity to search your heart and see whether or not you are truly presenting your best to the Lord — something that is costly and valuable (1 Chronicles 21:24).

It's this simple: If you want GOD'S best, make sure you are giving Him YOUR best. Don't just give Him the *leftovers* of your time, your talents, and your treasure. He gave *His* best to you, and He deserves no less than your best in return.

This passage in Malachi also shows an amazing connection between the quality of our sacrifices and our effectiveness in spreading God's glory to the nations:

*"For from the rising of the sun even to its setting, **My name will be great among the nations, and in every place incense is going to be offered to My name,** and a grain offering that is pure..." says the LORD of hosts.*

"Cursed be the swindler who has a male in his flock and vows it, but sacrifices a blemished animal to the Lord, for I am a great

*King," says the LORD of hosts, "and **My name is feared among the nations"** (1:11, 14 NASB).*

The Lord is a great King, and our commission to proclaim His name to the nations is fueled when we give Him our best — our sacrificial offerings. We must not stop until the name of Jesus is worshiped and proclaimed *"in every place"* and the earth is filled with the knowledge of His glory (Habakkuk 2:14).

12 PLUNDER THE EGYPTIANS

Passover was instituted by God as a wonderful time of forgiveness, protection, and new beginnings. This was to be *"an everlasting ordinance"* commemorating the deliverance of God's people from centuries of slavery in Egypt.

When I see all the blessings and breakthroughs offered to us in God's appointed times, I have a hard time understanding why *everyone* wouldn't be eager to participate. Are you in need of more assurance of God's forgiveness and favor today? Is there some difficult situation in your health, finances, emotions, or relationships that you need deliverance from? Have you come to the end of yourself, needing a new beginning in your life?

If there was nothing more to the story than God's offer of these amazing blessings, it would be stunning to say the least. But the Passover story includes much more than just getting the Israelites out of slavery, as fantastic as that was. Look at this additional feature of God's Passover blessings:

> *Now the children of Israel had done according to the word of Moses, and they had asked from the Egyptians articles of silver, articles of gold, and clothing. And the LORD had given the people favor in the sight of the Egyptians, so that they granted them what they requested. Thus they plundered the Egyptians*
> (Exodus 12:35-36).

First, we are told that the Israelites obeyed the Lord *"according to the word of Moses."* From that place of faith and obedience, they *"asked from the Egyptians articles of silver, articles of gold, and clothing."* For hundreds of years, the Egyptians had been their cruel captors, and now the Israelites were asking not just for *freedom*, but for *reparations* as well!

Because of their obedience to God's Passover instructions, the children of Israel knew they had His favor. But notice that the Lord's favor also resulted in *"favor in the sight of the Egyptians."*

What a beautiful principle we see here: When you have God's favor, He can give you favor with people as well—even people who have previously been your enemies! After the Israelites *"plundered the Egyptians,"* they left their captivity with unimaginable riches and prosperity. Instead of being paupers and beggars, they were abundantly provided with silver, gold, clothing, and *"a great deal of livestock"* (v. 38).

At the conclusion of the description of the first Passover, we're told, *"This is that night of the LORD, a solemn observance for all the children of Israel throughout their generations"* (v. 42). Not only were God's people enabled to plunder the ungodly Egyptians during that first Passover, but those same blessings are available when you observe His appointed times today.

Proverbs 13:22 promises, *"The wealth of the sinner is stored up for the righteous."* However, I've met many Christians who can quote that great promise, yet they seem unable to experience its fulfillment in their lives. Could it be that they need to return to what the Israelites *did* when they plundered the Egyptians during the first Passover celebration?

Remember: God has appointments to bless you. When you follow His instructions, you can confidently expect His amazing promises to be fulfilled in your life.

13 GIVE GOD YOUR FIRSTFRUITS

One of the most beautiful promises in the Bible is found in Paul's letter to the Romans: *"We know that God causes all things to work together for good to those who love God, to those who are called according to His purpose"* (Romans 8:28 NASB). Isn't it good to know that no matter what you may be going through today, God is able to turn it around and use it to bless you and fulfill His purposes?

The feasts God designated as His *"appointed times"* provide a powerful confirmation that He is willing and able to work out every circumstance for your good. Long before you were even born, the Lord put appointments on His calendar to bless you with extraordinary miracles and breakthroughs.

Be clear on this: The feasts of the Lord were not random events, happening in some kind of haphazard way. God was very precise about when He scheduled these appointed times. The timing was important to Him, and it should be important to us as well.

For example, the Feast of Firstfruits was a spring feast connected to Passover. Three days after Passover, the first sheaf of the barley harvest would be waved by the priests as an offering to the Lord. This event was a wonderful foreshadowing of Jesus' resurrection, three days after His crucifixion.

But the resurrection isn't the *only* Biblical event that happened on the *same day* as the Feast of Firstfruits, which is in the month of Nisan, the first month on the Jewish calendar:

- Noah's ark rested safely on Mount Ararat, signaling a new beginning for Noah's family and a fresh start for humanity (Genesis 8:4).

- After 430 years of captivity, the children of Israel were released from their slavery on the exact same day as they had first entered Egypt (Exodus 12:40-41).

- God parted the Red Sea and brought the Israelites safely to the other side (Exodus 3:18, 5:3).

- Israel ate the fruits of the Promised Land for the first time after crossing the Jordan River (Joshua 5:13).

- Queen Esther saved the Hebrew people from annihilation (Esther 3:12, 5:1).

The odds of all of these events randomly occurring on the same day of the Hebrew year would be astronomical. Yet God's sovereign hand orchestrates the affairs of His people to coincide with His appointed times and seasons.

My friend, you can entrust yourself to a faithful God today. Synchronize your life to fit into His special times and seasons to bless you. Yes, He can bless you *any* day, of course. But He has also specified appointed times when He will give you *extraordinary* blessings and breakthroughs.

And I encourage you not to miss the vital *"firstfruits"* principle found throughout the Scriptures. On the Feast of Firstfruits, God brought His Son Jesus up from the dead as *"the firstfruits of those who have fallen asleep"* (1 Corinthians 15:20-23). And just as God observed the law of

firstfruits, so He tells us that this is an indispensable key for receiving His blessings in our lives:

> *Honor the LORD with your possessions, and with the **firstfruits** of all your increase; so your barns will be filled with plenty, and your vats will overflow with new wine* (Proverbs 3:9-10).

Too often, Believers today give God their *leftovers* instead of their firstfruits — if they give Him anything at all. The average churchgoer in America gives God less than 2.5% of their income, far short of the tithe (10%) commanded in Malachi 3:10 or the special offerings He asks us to bring to Him during His *"appointed times,"* the feasts. Is it any wonder so many Believers are living below their inheritance, living in the land of NOT ENOUGH instead of the land of MORE THAN ENOUGH?

Give God your firstfruits, my friend, and then watch Him transform your life and your circumstances. Instead of poverty and struggles, you will find yourself *"filled with plenty,"* enjoying overflowing abundance from the bounty of your gracious Heavenly Father.

BE EMPOWERED BY THE SPIRIT 14

Many people read the story in Acts 2 about the outpouring of the Holy Spirit without giving any thought to the fact that it happened on one of God's appointed times — the Feast of Pentecost. This feast was a *"holy convocation"* celebrating the first fruits of the harvest in the Israelites' new Promised Land (Leviticus 23:15-17, Deuteronomy 26:1-11):

> *When you come into the land which the LORD your God is giving you as an inheritance, and you possess it and dwell in it, that you shall take some of the first of all the produce of the ground, which you shall bring from your land that the LORD your God is giving you...*
>
> *And you shall go to the one who is priest in those days, and say to him, "I declare today to the LORD your God that I have come to the country which the LORD swore to our fathers to give us"* (Deuteronomy 26:1-3).

Pentecost is also referred to as the "Feast of Weeks." It is observed in the third month of the Jewish calendar and during May/June on our current Gregorian calendar. "Pentecost" literally means "the 50th day," because this feast falls exactly 50 days following the Feast of Firstfruits (50 days from the first Sabbath after Passover).

During this special day, the Israelites were again told by God to give an offering of their first fruits, and they also were to bring two loaves of leavened bread before the Lord: *"You shall bring from your dwellings two wave loaves of two-tenths of an ephah. They shall be of fine flour; they shall be baked with leaven. They are the firstfruits to the LORD"* (Leviticus 23:17). These two loaves foreshadowed the Day of Pentecost in Acts 2, when Jews and Gentiles would be joined together as *"one new man"* (Ephesians 2:15).

Pentecost still has powerful significance today, extending far beyond the Israelites' celebration of the firstfruits of the Promised Land. But it's important for you to see the timeline on this.

Christ was crucified on the Feast of Passover, and He rose from the dead on the Feast of Firstfruits. For a period of 40 days, the risen Jesus taught His disciples about His Kingdom (Acts 1:3). He also reaffirmed His promise that they soon would be endued with *"power from on high"* and *"baptized with the Holy Spirit"* (Luke 24:49, Acts 1:4-5). Through the outpouring of the Spirit, they would be empowered to be Jesus' witnesses throughout the world (Acts 1:8).

Forty days after His resurrection, Jesus ascended into Heaven (Acts 1:9). Then for 10 days His followers waited and prayed, until the Spirit was finally poured out in very dramatic fashion:

> *When the Day of Pentecost had fully come, they were all with one accord in one place. And suddenly there came a sound from heaven, as of a rushing mighty wind, and it filled the whole house where they were sitting. Then there appeared to them divided tongues, as of fire, and one sat upon each of them. And they were all filled with the Holy Spirit and began to speak with other tongues, as the Spirit gave them utterance* (Acts 2:1-4).

This was the first Pentecost of the Church Age, exactly 50 days after Jesus' resurrection. On this appointed time on God's calendar, the church was born and filled with supernatural power to take the Gospel

to *"every tribe and language and people and nation"* (Revelation 5:9).

The Feast of Pentecost is also the day when the Jewish people traditionally celebrate God's giving of the Law to Moses on Mount Sinai (Exodus 20), which is recognized as the birthday of the nation of Israel. Do you see how significant this is? Israel and the church have the same birthday — the Day of Pentecost! From His people Israel and from His church, the Lord took Jews and Gentiles and formed them together into *"one new man"* as a testimony of His glory and grace!

Look at these other parallels and contrasts between the giving of the Law and the outpouring of the Holy Spirit:

- At Mount Sinai, the Law was written on tablets of *stone,* but in the New Covenant the Holy Spirit writes the Law on our *hearts* (Jeremiah 31:33).

- *Mount Sinai* was topped with fire when the Law was given (Deuteronomy 5:23-25), but in Acts 2:3 the fire rested upon the *Believers.*

- While the Law was given at *Mount Sinai,* the Holy Spirit was poured out on *Mount Zion* (Jerusalem).

- At *Mount Sinai, 3,000 people were slain* because of their idolatry and disobedience (Exodus 33:25-28), but on the Day of Pentecost in Acts, *3,000 people were saved* when they heard Peter preach the Gospel (Acts 2:41).

- When Exodus 20 and Acts 2 are combined, we see a beautiful picture of the two primary ways that the Lord wants to guide His people: by His *Word* and by His *Spirit!*

I encourage you to pause right now and thank the Lord for the power of His Spirit, poured out for YOU at Pentecost. There's no need to feel weak or powerless in your Christian life. God has sent you *"power from on high,"* enabling you to be a fruitful witness for Christ.

15 RECOGNIZE GOD'S PROPHETIC PLAN

Why should Believers today study the feasts God prescribed as His appointed times? There are numerous reasons, as we've already seen.

First of all, you should study the feasts because the Bible describes how important they are to Him. If something is important to HIM, shouldn't it be important to YOU as well?

Second, it's vital to understand the feasts so you can grow in your intimacy with the Lord and receive more of his covenant blessings in your life.

And the third reason to study the feasts is to gain a greater appreciation for God's prophetic plan. You see, the springtime feasts of Passover, Unleavened Bread, Firstfruits, and Pentecost all speak primarily of prophetic events that have already been fulfilled:

- **Passover** was a prophetic foreshadow of Jesus as *"the Lamb of God"* (John 1:29, 1 Corinthians 5:7).

- **Unleavened Bread** was a prophetic foreshadow of Jesus' sinless life and His identity as *"the bread of God...who comes down from heaven and gives life to the world"* (John 6:33).

- **Firstfruits** was a prophetic foreshadow of the resurrected

Christ as *"the firstfruits of those who have fallen asleep"* (1 Corinthians 15:20).

- **Pentecost** was a prophetic foreshadow of the outpouring of the Holy Spirit, joining the Jews and Gentiles together as one body, empowered as witnesses for Christ (Acts 2:1-4).

However, just as the four spring feasts pointed to events that have already been fulfilled by Jesus or in the early church, the three fall feasts all point prophetically to events that are still in the future:

- **Feast of Trumpets** (Leviticus 23:24) appears to be associated with the return of Christ, which will be accompanied by a loud trumpet sound (1 Thessalonians 4:13-18, Revelation 11:15). Even though we don't know the exact day or hour of our Lord's return, it seems likely He will come back during the season of the Feast of Trumpets. It is significant that the final trumpet during this feast is called "Tekia HaGedolah," which means "the last or great trumpet." Paul seems to be referring to this prophetic season when he writes, *"Behold, I tell you a mystery: We shall not all sleep, but we shall all be changed — in a moment, in the twinkling of an eye, at the last trumpet. For the trumpet will sound, and the dead will be raised incorruptible, and we shall be changed"* (1 Corinthians 15:51-52).

  Remember that Paul was a Jew, and He was writing primarily to people familiar with the Hebrew Scriptures. When he wrote here about *"the last trumpet"* or of *"the trumpet of God"* that will sound when Christ returns (1 Thessalonians 4:13-5:1-5), his readers fully understood that he was referring to the imagery of the Feast of Trumpets.

- **Day of Atonement** (Leviticus 16, 23:27) sometimes is seen as a prophetic foreshadow of the final judgment. It's interesting that the Day of Atonement (*Yom Kippur*) comes immediately

after the Feast of Trumpets (*Rosh Hashanah,* "Head of the Year"). After the *"last trumpet"* sounds, there will be a time of judgment, followed by the beginning of Christ's eternal reign. Instead of just being the beginning of a *new year,* this will be the start of a *whole new age* for humanity.

- **Feast of Tabernacles** (Leviticus 23:34) looks back at God's faithfulness to Israel in the wilderness, but also looks ahead prophetically to the Millennial Kingdom, when God's people in all the nations will *continue* to celebrate this feast (Zechariah 14:16-19, Micah 4:1-7).

You see, my friend, God has already fulfilled the prophetic pattern of each of the spring feasts, and I'm convinced Jesus will return soon to signal the fulfillment of the fall feasts as well. Are you ready for that day? Do you have assurance of your salvation and an eagerness to greet your Savior when He returns?

Please pause and take a few moments to examine your heart before the Lord. Make sure your sins have been forgiven and you are walking in obedient fellowship with God.

As the fall feasts so beautifully illustrate, the trumpet will soon sound, declaring Christ's return. *"Surely I am coming quickly,"* He says (Revelation 22:20). May your wholehearted reply be this: *"Even so, come, Lord Jesus!"*

BE REMINDED OF GOD'S FAITHFULNESS 16

Have you ever needed a reminder? I'm sure you have. We *all* have at one time or another.

Perhaps you needed a reminder of an appointment with a friend or a special day like a birthday or anniversary. Or maybe you had to be reminded it was time for your annual medical checkup or the regular oil change for your car.

One of the great blessings of God's feast days is that they serve as powerful reminders of His love and faithfulness. When you observe the feasts each year, you are reminded of His complete redemptive plan, and you can gain access to His amazing promises of blessing and provision.

- When you celebrate the **Feast of Passover**…you're reminded of the blood of Jesus that purchased your forgiveness and cleansed you from every sin. It's a time of *new beginnings* for you! And you can rejoice that because of the blood on the doorposts of your heart and life, the evil one no longer has any right to torment you (Revelation 12:10-11).

- When you observe the **Feast of Unleavened Bread** (which is part of the Passover celebration)…you are reminded of Jesus' sinless life and His desire to set you free from any

besetting sins (1 Corinthians 5:7-8).

- When you think of the **Feast of Firstfruits**…you're reminded of Jesus' resurrection from the dead and the fact that His resurrection power now lives in YOU (Romans 8:11).

- When you remember the **Feast of Pentecost**…you're reminded that Jews and Gentiles have been joined together as *"one new man"* (Ephesians 2:15), and you can rejoice that the Holy Spirit has empowered you to be a bold witness for Christ (Acts 1:8).

- When you reflect on the **Feast of Trumpets** (*Rosh Hashanah*) …you can rejoice that Christ will soon return, heralded with a loud trumpet blast (1 Thessalonians 4:13-18, 1 Corinthians 15:51-55, Revelation 11:15). No matter what you may be going through today, you can lift up your head, *"because your redemption draws near"* (Luke 21:28).

- When you observe the **Day of Atonement**…you can remember the atonement won for you by Jesus on the cross. You can come boldly to God's throne of grace to *"obtain mercy and find grace to help in time of need"* (Hebrews 4:16). And you can have confidence that you will stand victoriously before *"the judgment seat of Christ"* after you die (2 Corinthians 5:10).

- When you celebrate the **Feast of Tabernacles**…you are reminded of God's loving care and provision for the Israelites during their sojourn to the Promised Land, and you can claim His promises for an abundant life *today* (John 10:10).

Do you see why these special times on God's calendar can be such a

blessing and encouragement to you today? Whether you need for-giveness, financial provision, a physical healing, deliverance from an addiction, peace of mind, or the restoration of a relationship, these are appointed times for your breakthrough!

Sometimes it's *humbling* to acknowledge that we need reminders, but we DO! The apostle Peter wrote that both of his epistles were *"reminders to hold your minds in a state of undistracted attention"* (2 Peter 3:1 MSG).

I'm convinced that God's appointed times were designed to remind you…provide for you…and draw you into a covenant relationship of greater intimacy with Him. Don't miss your appointments. They can be times of extraordinary blessing and favor in your life.

17 Do This in Remembrance

Often people celebrate Holy Communion or "the Lord's Supper" today without giving any thought to the fact that this observance was originally connected to the Feast of Passover. Jesus didn't institute Communion as a totally new event, but rather it was first celebrated as He was eating the final Passover meal with His disciples before His death.

Look at how the apostle Paul described the scene:

> *I received from the Lord that which I also delivered to you: that the Lord Jesus on the same night in which He was betrayed took bread; and when He had given thanks, He broke it and said, "Take, eat; this is My body which is broken for you; do this in remembrance of Me." In the same manner He also took the cup after supper, saying, "This cup is the new covenant in My blood. This do, as often as you drink it, in remembrance of Me"* (1 Corinthians 11:23-25).

As we saw in the last chapter, the Lord's feasts are meant to remind us of His love and faithfulness, but this passage brings out another vital principle: *Passover and the other feasts are meant to point us to JESUS!* Our Savior plainly said we're to celebrate Passover in a new way: *"…in remembrance of Me."*

While the blood of the Passover lamb pointed to the *"lamb of God"* who would one day come, Jesus IS that lamb! Every element of the Passover ceremony foreshadowed God's redemptive plan, ultimately culminating with the *"new covenant"* enacted through Jesus' blood.

I love the next line of this passage: *"For as often as you eat this bread and drink this cup, you proclaim the Lord's death till He comes"* (v. 26). When you celebrate Passover in light of Holy Communion, you are doing several distinct things:

- ***Looking back*** to commemorate what Jesus did for you on the cross.

- ***Looking forward*** to the day when He will return to take you home with Him for all eternity.

- ***Recognizing His abiding presence with you NOW,*** as the One who *"will never leave you nor forsake you"* (Hebrews 13:5).

What a beautiful testimony to the fact that *"Jesus Christ is the same yesterday, today, and forever"* (Hebrews 13:8). He truly is *"the Alpha and the Omega, the Beginning and the End…who is and who was and who is to come, the Almighty"* (Revelation 1:8).

In the context of explaining the blessings of the Lord's Supper in 1 Corinthians 11:17-34, Paul also warns against partaking of the emblems of the Lord's body and blood *"in an unworthy manner"* (v. 27). Instead, we must examine ourselves (v. 28). Paul makes the sobering conclusion that many people in the Corinthian church were weak, sick, or even had died because of abusing this special time to celebrate the Lord (v. 30). Sadly, they had missed out on the blessings available through properly observing this extremely important occasion.

My friend, whenever you celebrate Passover, Communion, or any of God's feasts, make sure you are doing so with your focus on Jesus and all He has done for you. In order to keep your observances from

turning into empty religious rituals, be sure your actions are *"in remembrance"* of HIM.

This same principle applies to how you read the Scriptures. *The Message* paraphrases Jesus' words in John 5:39: "*You have your heads in your Bibles constantly because you think you'll find eternal life there. But you miss the forest for the trees. These Scriptures are all about **me**!*"

Yes, you should diligently study the Bible in order to know and do what it says. But all the while, you should keep in mind that Jesus is the focal point of everything written in God's Word. As John was told in his heavenly vision, *"The testimony of Jesus is the spirit of prophecy"* (Revelation 19:10).

That's why the feasts can be such a blessing, my friend — because they all testify of Jesus and His great redemptive work on your behalf. Christ is our Passover and the Unleavened Bread that purifies us from sin. He is the giver of the Holy Spirit at Pentecost and the coming King whose arrival is announced by the blast of trumpets. He "tabernacled" among us during His first coming (John 1:14), and soon He will tabernacle among us as the King of kings for all eternity (Revelation 21:3).

Instructions for Your Turnaround 18

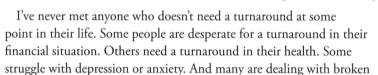

I've never met anyone who doesn't need a turnaround at some point in their life. Some people are desperate for a turnaround in their financial situation. Others need a turnaround in their health. Some struggle with depression or anxiety. And many are dealing with broken relationships in their family.

What kind of turnaround do *you* need today? The good news is that your Heavenly Father *specializes* in turnarounds and breakthroughs. He only asks that you follow *His instructions.*

Over and over again, Jesus' disciples learned the necessity of following His instructions — even if they didn't understand the *reason* for the instructions at first. Why should they let down their fishing nets when they had already fished all night and caught nothing? Why should they be foolhardy enough to attempt to feed thousands of hungry people with just five loaves and two fish? And why, when they needed money for taxes, should they look for a coin in the mouth of a fish?

But over the months and years, the disciples learned to trust and obey Jesus whenever He told them to do something. When they followed His instructions, good things happened!

When it was time to celebrate the Feast of Passover, the disciples knew this was an event Jesus would never miss. The only question was

one of logistics: *"**Where** do you want us to make preparations for you to eat the Passover?"* they asked (Matthew 26:17 NIV).

Notice that they never asked Jesus IF He was going to celebrate Passover. Their only question was WHERE. The Bible is absolutely clear that Jesus celebrated the feasts…the disciples celebrated the feasts… Paul celebrated the feasts…and the early church celebrated the feasts!

To the disciples' question, Jesus replied, *"Go into the city to a certain man and tell him, 'The Teacher says: **My appointed time is near.** I am going to celebrate the **Passover** with my disciples at your house.' **So the disciples did as Jesus had directed them and prepared the Passover"*** (vs. 18-19 NIV).

Jesus said He had an appointment to keep. It wasn't just any old appointment, for He referred to it as *"My appointed time."* If Jesus told you to meet Him at a certain time and place in order to receive incredible miracles and breakthroughs in your life, I bet you would make sure to be there…and *on time!* I surely would.

And I love the description of the disciples' faithfulness to Jesus' instructions: *"So the disciples **did** as Jesus had directed them and prepared the Passover."*

My friend, if you need a turnaround today, I ask you to examine your heart and make sure you've been following the Lord's instructions. Perhaps He is directing YOU to prepare the Passover or carry out some other command of Scripture.

Like the disciples, you may not initially see how Jesus' instructions will improve your life or lead to your turnaround. But remember this: God instituted the Feast of Passover when He led His people out of slavery in Egypt to begin their journey to the Promised Land, *"a land flowing with milk and honey"* (Exodus 13:3-5). What an amazing turnaround it was! From slavery to freedom. From poverty

to prosperity. From the land of NOT ENOUGH to the land of MORE THAN ENOUGH!

Just as God supernaturally intervened to bless the children of Israel during Passover, He wants to stretch out His mighty hand to bring you into His land of abundance today. Whatever turnaround you need, your special season of blessings can begin when you honor God and do as He asks.

19 BLESSINGS OF THE NEW COVENANT

When Jesus celebrated His final Passover meal with His disciples, He explained to them that He was instituting *"the new covenant in My blood"* (Luke 22:20). It's important for us to understand the incredible blessings included in this new covenant, which was described by the prophet Jeremiah hundreds of years before Jesus was even born:

> *Behold, the days are coming, says the LORD, when I will make a new covenant with the house of Israel and with the house of Judah — not according to the covenant that I made with their fathers in the day that I took them by the hand to lead them out of the land of Egypt, My covenant which they broke, though I was a husband to them, says the LORD.*

> *But this is the covenant that I will make with the house of Israel after those days, says the LORD: I will put My law in their minds, and write it on their hearts; and I will be their God, and they shall be My people. No more shall every man teach his neighbor, and every man his brother, saying, "Know the LORD," for they all shall know Me, from the least of them to the greatest of them, says the LORD. For I will forgive their iniquity, and their sin I will remember no more* (Jeremiah 31:31-34).

This passage is loaded with vital insights about the new covenant,

but four specific points stand out:

1. ***God puts His law in our heart.*** Under the old covenant, the Law was primarily external, written by God on stone tablets and given to Moses at Mount Sinai. But under the new covenant, the Law is imprinted by the Holy Spirit on our hearts when we give our life to Christ.

2. ***God will be our God, and we shall be His people.*** This is covenant language, describing a permanent, unbreakable bond between the Lord and His people.

3. ***God will reveal Himself to every Believer, personally and intimately.*** Instead of just being *taught* about God, we can have an intimate *relationship* with Him. And you don't have to be a king, a priest, a prophet or anyone "special," because God says, *"ALL shall know Me, from the least of them to the greatest of them."*

4. ***God will forgive our sins fully and forever.*** No longer will our guilt or shame get in the way of having a relationship with God. Our forgiveness will be so complete that God says he won't even *remember* our sins anymore! Instead of hanging over our head forever, our sins will be cast *"into the depths of the sea"* (Micah 7:19).

As part of the new covenant, you can have total security in your relationship with God. Rather than being unreliable, like human love often is, the Lord provides this beautiful assurance concerning His love for you: *"I have loved you with an everlasting love"* (Jeremiah 31:3).

Isn't that great news? You don't have to be in doubt about your salvation or about God's love for you. As He repeatedly demonstrated to the Israelites throughout their history, His love is faithful and true. If you are in Christ, there is no longer any condemnation, and *nothing*

can separate you from God's love for you (Romans 8:1, 33-39).

This doesn't mean life will always be carefree or easy. Jeremiah, who had such a great revelation of the new covenant, was deeply distressed when his beloved city of Jerusalem was ransacked by the Babylonians. But even in that dark hour, he was able to encourage himself by remembering God's faithful covenant love:

> *This I recall to my mind,*
> *Therefore I have hope.*
> *Through the LORD's mercies we are not consumed,*
> *Because His compassions fail not.*
> *They are new every morning;*
> *Great is Your faithfulness.*
> *"The LORD is my portion," says my soul,*
> *"Therefore I hope in Him!"* (Lamentations 3:21-24)

My friend, each time you observe one of God's appointed times, you have an opportunity to thank Him for His covenant love. No matter what you may be going through today, you can remember that His mercies are *"new every morning."* You can put your hope in Him and declare in faith, *"Great is Your faithfulness!"*

WHAT ABOUT THE LAW?

Often people get confused about why we should continue to celebrate God's prescribed feasts, even though a new covenant was instituted by Jesus' death and resurrection. Sometimes people tell me, "David, the feasts and God's other commandments were just under the Law. Now we're living under grace in a new covenant, and such things are obsolete and irrelevant."

Yes, my friend, we *are* living under grace. But the Bible says God's appointed times are to be observed *forever.* Passover, Pentecost, and Tabernacles are not just Old Testament religious observances, but rather they are God-ordained times of blessing for Believers throughout every generation. These three feasts are special times to God, and because of that, they should be special to you and me as well!

While keeping God's holy convocations has nothing to do with your salvation, celebrating these special days *will* enable you to reap His harvest blessings in a greater magnitude and dimension than you've ever experienced before. Rather than bringing about "bondage" to the Law, God's celebrations will bring you His BLESSINGS.

Right from the beginning of Jesus' ministry, people have had questions about how His new covenant would impact their responsibilities under the Law. Our Lord addressed these questions quite directly:

> *Do not think that I came to destroy the Law or the Prophets. I did not come to destroy but to fulfill. For assuredly, I say to you, till heaven and earth pass away, one jot or one tittle will by no means pass from the law till all is fulfilled* (Matthew 5:17-18).

Of course, many things have changed under the new covenant. For example, you no longer need to sacrifice animals to atone for your sins, because Jesus already paid that price through the blood He shed for you on the cross.

However, when you think of other precepts of the Law — such as prohibitions against murder, stealing, or adultery — it's obvious that God still expects such rules to be followed. Why? Because they express His will and illustrate what it means to live a life pleasing to Him.

Yes, there is a new and better covenant, but it's also true that God never changes (Malachi 3:6). Our Lord is *"the same yesterday, today, and forever"* (Hebrews 13:8), so you can see patterns throughout His Word of the things that please Him and the things that anger Him.

Many Biblical principles for a life of abundance were set in place before the Law was instituted on Mount Sinai in Exodus 20. For example, Abraham first paid tithes hundreds of years *before* the Law was given (Genesis 14:20). And the Feast of Passover was commanded by God in Exodus 12 — when the Israelites were still in Egypt — and the Law wasn't given until after they escaped Egypt and passed through the Red Sea.

So it's obvious that the feasts weren't primarily tied to the Law. God simply told us to remember His special days. Just as you would remember your own anniversary or the birthdays of your loved ones and friends, is God asking too much when He says to celebrate the appointed times on His calendar? Instead of just being an obligation or duty, this should be part of your love relationship with the Lord. Not drudgery, but delight.

Why not trust the Lord and take a step of faith to honor His *"appointed times,"* my friend? When you do, you can expect exciting things to happen!

21 YOUR KEY TO SPIRITUAL BREAKTHROUGHS

Throughout the history of Israel, there were many ups and downs in their relationship with the Lord. God's people often strayed from His ways, and repentance was needed in order to spark a new beginning of His blessings and favor.

King Hezekiah's father, Ahaz, had been *"increasingly unfaithful to the LORD"* (2 Chronicles 28:22). Instead of leading the people closer to the Lord, He took them down the path of pagan idolatry, *"to burn incense to other gods"* (v. 25). Predictably, God was angry!

When King Ahaz died, Hezekiah became king, and *"he did what was right in the sight of the LORD, according to all that his father David had done"* (2 Chronicles 29:1-2). What did this include? First, Hezekiah repaired and cleansed the temple, and *"the service of the house of the LORD was set in order"* (v. 35).

My friend, take a moment and consider how this story may apply to your life at this point. Have you been *"unfaithful to the LORD"* in some way? Have you allowed some kind of idolatry to creep into your heart and life? Are there some areas of your life that God wants to *"set in order"*?

It's interesting that one of the things Hezekiah set in order was the observance of Passover and God's other *"appointed times."* We read in

2 Chronicles 30:1 that *"Hezekiah sent to all Israel and Judah…that they should come to the house of the LORD at Jerusalem, to keep the Passover to the LORD God of Israel."*

This is pretty stunning, isn't it? Of all the reforms Hezekiah could have made after the disastrous reign of his father, one of the first things he did was to reestablish the celebration of Passover. This was no easy task, *"since they had not done it for a long time in the prescribed manner"* (v. 5).

Sadly, the same could be said of most of the church today. For most Christians, they haven't celebrated the feasts of the Lord *"for a long time"* — if at all.

Hezekiah sent runners throughout the land to command his people, *"Children of Israel, return to the LORD God of Abraham, Isaac, and Israel; then He will return to the remnant of you who have escaped from the hand of the kings of Assyria"* (v. 6). Notice that this command to celebrate Passover was framed in terms of returning to the LORD. In order to fully return to a place of God's favor, they had to obey Him by returning to His appointed times.

Hezekiah's message warned, *"Now do not be stiff-necked, as your fathers were, but yield yourselves to the Lord"* (v. 8). This is significant, because the previous generation had followed Ahaz and other unfaithful kings into idolatry. It was going to take a real *decision* for the people to break with that sinful tradition and yield to the Lord.

Hezekiah's messengers did not have an easy time. Instead of immediately embracing this message of repentance and restoration from the king's envoys, *"they laughed at them and mocked them"* (v. 10). As someone who has tried to trumpet this message about God's desire to bless His people through celebrating His feasts once again, I can sympathize with these messengers. Many people still mock anyone who declares that God's appointed times are still relevant today.

Fortunately, Hezekiah was not deterred from this response, and eventually the Lord convinced some people to join in the Passover restoration: *"The hand of God was on Judah to give them singleness of heart to obey the command of the king and the leaders, at the word of the LORD"* (v. 12). Eventually, *"a very great assembly"* gathered in Jerusalem to celebrate Passover.

As the massive congregation prepared their hearts to seek God, we're told that the Lord *"healed the people"* (vs. 19-20) and brought them *"great gladness"* (v. 21). The outpouring of blessings and joy was so overwhelming that *"the whole assembly agreed to keep the feast another seven days"* (v. 23).

What an amazing scene! Because of their disobedience, it had been a long time since God's people had celebrated Passover. But once they did, somewhat reluctantly for some, the blessings were so evident that they extended the celebration for an additional seven days! As the chapter ends, we're told that the Levites *"arose and blessed the people, and their voice was heard; and their prayer came up to His holy dwelling place, to heaven"* (v. 27).

What a beautiful testimony. As you set your heart to obey the Lord and honor Him during His appointed times, you will be *blessed,* and your prayers will ascend all the way to Heaven!

DO YOU NEED A HEALING? 22

When God instituted His three *"appointed times"* in Exodus 23, He specifically listed good health and a long life as part of the blessings you can receive:

> *You shall serve the LORD your God, and He will bless your bread and your water. And I will take sickness away from the midst of you. No one shall suffer miscarriage or be barren in your land; I will fulfill the number of your days* (vs. 25-26).

If you or a loved one is in need of healing today, I encourage you to take these great promises to heart. When you are faithful to God's requirements, He promises to take away sickness…eliminate miscarriages and infertility…and *"fulfill the number of your days."* In the New Living Translation, the Lord says, *"I will give you long, full lives."*

God promises these things in the context of stating the benefits of celebrating the feasts of Passover, Pentecost, and Tabernacles, but He had already made a similar statement shortly after the Israelites left Egypt:

> *If you diligently heed the voice of the LORD your God and do what is right in His sight, give ear to His commandments and keep all His statutes, I will put none of the diseases on you which I have brought on the Egyptians. For I am the LORD who heals you* (Exodus 15:26).

My friend, God wants to be your Healer and Great Physician today. But the healing process comes when you heed His voice and follow His commandments.

King Hezekiah was a man who did this. One of his greatest accomplishments was restoring the Passover celebrations to Israel — something that had been neglected before his reign. Hezekiah had been faithful to the Lord, and when he needed a miracle, God answered him and came to his aid:

> *In those days Hezekiah was sick and near death. And Isaiah the prophet, the son of Amoz, went to him and said to him, "Thus says the LORD: 'Set your house in order, for you shall die and not live.'"*

> *Then Hezekiah turned his face toward the wall, and prayed to the LORD, and said, "Remember now, O LORD, I pray, how I have walked before You in truth and with a loyal heart, and have done what is good in Your sight." And Hezekiah wept bitterly.*

> *And the word of the LORD came to Isaiah, saying, "Go and tell Hezekiah, 'Thus says the LORD, the God of David your father: "I have heard your prayer, I have seen your tears; surely I will add to your days fifteen years"'"* (Isaiah 38:1-5).

When it looked as if Hezekiah was about to die, he reminded the Lord of his "loyal heart." God heard his prayer and sent the prophet Isaiah to declare, "I will add to your days fifteen years."

In addition to healing Hezekiah and extending his life, God had even more blessings in store for him: *"I will deliver you and this city from the hand of the king of Assyria, and I will defend this city"* (v. 6). You see, one of God's great blessings for those who observe His special feasts is this: *"I will be an enemy to your enemies and an adversary to*

your adversaries" (Exodus 23:22). Because of Hezekiah's faithfulness to celebrate the *"appointed times,"* he could be assured of overwhelming victory over his enemies.

If all this wasn't enough, God went on to give Hezekiah a stunning display of His supernatural favor: *"Behold, I will bring the shadow on the sundial, which has gone down with the sun on the sundial of Ahaz, ten degrees backward"* (Isaiah 38:8).

My friend, you serve a God who is so powerful that He can even turn back the shadow on a sundial — extending your life and turning back the hands of time on your behalf. He loves you more than you can imagine, and He longs to release His favor as you honor Him during His *"appointed times."*

23 RISE TOWARD GOD'S PRESENCE

One day I was reading my Bible and pouring over the book of Psalms, and my attention was caught by the little descriptive captions at the beginning of each psalm. Some of them read "A Psalm of David" or "To the Chief Musician." But when I got to Psalm 120, I started seeing captions I didn't understand.

All 15 captions for Psalm 120 through Psalm 134 said the same thing: "A Song of Ascents." Although I knew what "A Psalm of David" was, I was puzzled by the term "Psalm of Ascent." So I decided to do some digging into the meaning of this intriguing description.

The Hebrew word for "psalm" is *mizmor,* which means "a poem sung with instruments." Its root is another Hebrew word, *zamar,* which means "to touch the strings or parts of a musical instrument; to play upon; to make music accompanied by the voice; to praise." So a psalm is a song that is sung accompanied by musical instruments.

But what *"ascent"* was this description referring to? According to scholars, there are two answers to this.

First of all, these psalms were sung by worshipers each year as they ascended the road to Jerusalem to attend the three *"appointed time"* feasts: Passover, Pentecost, and Tabernacles. The intensity and anticipation built as each new psalm was sung on their way to meet with the

Lord during these special occasions.

The second use of these psalms was by the priests as they ascended the 15 steps to minister at the temple. After a priest had performed a sacrifice on the bronze altar and washed in the bronze laver in the outer court, he came to a set of stairs leading up to the temple, which housed the inner court and Holy of Holies.

As the priest stood before these steps, he would sing Psalm 120: *"In my trouble, I cried to the Lord, and He answered me. Deliver my soul, oh Lord, from lying lips, from a deceitful tongue…"* (Psalm 120:1-2). Perhaps YOU are in some kind of trouble or distress today — whether in your finances, your health, your relationships, or your peace of mind. God wants you to know that He sees what you are going through, and He wants to set you free from your distress as you honor Him today.

The priest would continue on, step by step for the next 14 steps, until he reached the inner court. Each step includes a powerful message of encouragement for your life today:

- **Step 1:** *"I will lift up my eyes to the mountains, from where shall my help come? My help comes from the Lord, who made Heaven and Earth…"* (Psalm 121:1-2).

- **Step 2:** *"I was glad when they said to me, 'Let us go to the house of the Lord…'"* (Psalm 122:1).

- **Step 3:** *"To You I lift up my eyes, oh You who are enthroned in the heavens…"* (Psalm 123:1).

- **Step 4:** *"Had it not been the Lord who was on our side when men rose up against us, then they would have swallowed us alive…the waters would have engulfed us…"* (Psalm 124:2, 4).

- **Step 5:** *"Those who trust in the Lord are as Mount Zion, which cannot be moved, but abides forever…"* (Psalm 125:1).

- **Step 6:** *"When the Lord brought back the captive ones of Zion, we were like those who dream. Then our mouth was filled with laughter and our tongue with joyful shouting…"* (Psalm 126:1-2).

- **Step 7:** *"Unless the Lord builds the house, they labor in vain who build it. Unless the Lord guards the city, the watchman keeps awake in vain…"* (Psalm 127:1).

- **Step 8:** *"How blessed is everyone who fears the Lord, who walks in His ways…"* (Psalms 128:1).

- **Step 9:** *"Many times they have persecuted me from my youth…"* (Psalm 129:1).

- **Step 10:** *"Out of the depths I have cried to You, O Lord. Lord, hear my voice…"* (Psalm 130:1-2).

- **Step 11:** *"O Lord, my heart is not proud, nor my eyes haughty, nor do I involve myself in great matters, or in things too difficult for me…"* (Psalm 131:1).

- **Step 12:** *"Remember, O Lord, on David's behalf, all his affliction; how he swore to the Lord and vowed to the Mighty One of Jacob…"* (Psalm 132:1-2).

- **Step 13:** *"Behold, how good and how pleasant it is for brothers to dwell together in unity…"* (Psalm 133:1).

- **Step 14:** *"Behold, bless the Lord, all servants of the Lord, who serve by night in the house of the Lord!"* (Psalm 134:1).

For the sake of space, I've only included the first one or two verses from each of the Psalms of Ascent, but I encourage you to read through all of them in your Bible. Just as they were an integral part of God's *"appointed times"* and the priests' ascension up the stairs into God's presence, so will the Lord use these psalms to draw you closer to Him.

Remember: God doesn't *need* you to praise Him. *YOU* need to praise Him, because in praising Him, you find blessings and victory. In His presence is *"fullness of joy"* (Psalm 16:11), and in His presence we are increasingly transformed into His likeness (2 Corinthians 3:18).

Just as the pilgrims on their way to celebrate the feasts knew they were approaching God's awesome presence, that should be your objective as well: meeting with God during His appointed times in order to gain greater intimacy with Him.

And as we see the example of the priests climbing the steps one at a time, singing God's praises and declaring Israel's desperate need for Him, so must you take steps of praise every day as you acknowledge that your hope is in Him alone. After all, as a Believer, YOU are a priest too, part of *"a royal priesthood, a holy nation, a people for God's own possession"* (1 Peter 2:9).

My friend, the final "Psalm of Ascent" is Psalm 134, and it ends with this triumphant reminder of your Heavenly Father's desire to draw you into His presence so He can BLESS you: *"The LORD who made heaven and earth **bless you** from Zion!"* (v. 3).

God is eager to bless you. Make sure you don't miss your appointment!

24 A CLOSER LOOK AT THE PSALMS OF ASCENT

In the last chapter, I shared some of the beautiful truths contained in Psalms 120 to 134, known as the "Psalms of Ascent." These psalms were sung by worshipers each year as they ascended the road to Jerusalem to attend the three *"appointed time"* feasts: Passover, Pentecost, and Tabernacles. The powerful truths contained in these psalms got the people of God ready to receive miracles from Him as they celebrated the feasts.

As we take a closer look at these psalms, picture yourself walking the road to Jerusalem, eagerly anticipating what God will do in your life. As you consider each psalm, your anticipation and faith grows for the breakthrough you need.

After the psalmist describes his troubles and distress in Psalm 120, we learn in Psalm 121 that the Lord is our Helper and our Keeper, the one who will keep us safe from all evil. So if the devil has been harassing you lately, remember that you can find safety today as you draw near to the Lord and ascend the pathway into His presence.

Psalm 122 says God wants to give you *prosperity* and *peace* as you come before Him. This was such a great promise to God's people as they obeyed Him and observed the three *"appointed times"* He had set for them.

Psalm 123 reminds us to *"look to the LORD our God"* (v. 2), trusting Him for our provision instead of looking to our jobs, the government, or the world's economic system. God set the three feasts as annual reminders that we must look to HIM as our Source.

I especially love Psalm 124, where David says Israel surely would have perished *"if it had not been the LORD who was on our side"* (vs. 1-3). I don't know what kind of battle you may be facing today, or what enemies you may be battling. But you can know this, my friend: If God is for you, no one can stand against you (Romans 8:31). One of His specific covenant promises is that He will be an enemy to your enemies (Exodus 23:22).

Psalm 125 paints a beautiful picture of God's protection in our lives, saying that He surrounds His people like the mountains surround Jerusalem (vs. 1-2). He is our Great Defender, and He will never leave us or forsake us (Hebrews 13:5).

Psalm 126 describes the Lord setting captives free and filling their mouths with laughter and singing (vs. 1-4). Perhaps this applies to you or a loved one today. God can set a person free from any form of addiction, replacing their bondage with His peace and joy.

Psalm 126 goes on to say we should declare that *"the LORD has done great things for us, and we are glad"* (v. 3). And HOW is it that He does these great things? Verse 5 explains: *"Those who sow in tears shall reap in joy."* The result of learning God's law of seedtime and harvest is that the world will look at you and say, "The Lord has done great things for them!" Hallelujah! I want that to be true of me, don't you?

Psalm 127 tells us the Lord *"gives His beloved sleep"* (v. 2), a wonderful promise of rest and security. It then speaks of the blessings God wants to put on the lives of our children and grandchildren: *"Children are a heritage from the LORD…they shall not be ashamed"* (vs. 3-5). This is a great reminder that God sees your concern for your loved ones,

my friend. He will intervene in their lives and replace their shame and defeat with His deliverance and victory.

Psalm 128 promises that when you walk in God's ways, *"You shall be happy, and it shall be well with you"* (v. 2). I don't know about you, but I NEED God's favor in my life. I NEED it to *"be well"* with me in the decisions I make today, in my relationships, and in the way I use my time, talent, and treasure. Remember, my friend: Your Heavenly Father has promised to give YOU this amazing favor as you walk in His ways.

Psalm 129 describes God's promises to give us healing, justice, and victory when we've been afflicted. Our enemies will *"be put to shame and turned back"* (v. 5).

Psalm 130 tells us that, even if we spend times in *"the depths"* (v. 1), we're promised God's *"abundant redemption"* (v. 7), forgiveness, mercy, and hope.

In Psalm 131, God encourages us that He can calm and quiet our soul. No matter what you may be going through today, He wants you to entrust your life to Him and discover His place of peace and safety, *"like a weaned child with his mother"* (v. 2).

In Psalm 132, God beckons us to draw near to Him and *"worship at His footstool"* (v. 7). When we do, we can *"shout for joy"* (v. 9), for God has promised to satisfy us with abundant provision (v. 15).

Psalm 133 describes the blessings we receive when the Lord brings us into unity with our loved ones and other believers. What an important reminder that God can give us breakthroughs in our relationships when we honor and obey Him.

When we reach Psalm 134, the final "Psalm of Ascent," we've almost arrived at our destination. We're told it's time to *"bless the Lord"* with our praise and worship! So I encourage you to stop and do that right now. Lift your voice to the Lord and thank Him in advance for what

He's about to do in your life!

As the Israelites sang the Psalms of Ascent, their hearts were prepared to receive God's covenant blessings during the Feasts of Passover, Pentecost, and Tabernacles. Remember that ALL of these blessings I've described from the Psalms of Ascent are based on God's people journeying to honor Him with their special offering during His feasts. Can you imagine the incredible sense of anticipation they must have had as they sang and recited these amazing promises during their journey?

May God stir your faith in a similar way today as you prepare to meet with Him. Expectancy is the breeding ground of His miracles and provision, and expectancy must be based on the promises in His Word. Get ready to be blessed!

25 MELT AWAY YOUR TROUBLES

When I meet Believers who refuse to acknowledge the value of celebrating God's *"appointed times,"* I'm both puzzled and saddened. I'm puzzled, because God told us so clearly to celebrate Passover, Pentecost, and Tabernacles *forever.* Shouldn't we all want to obey the Lord in this?

I'm also saddened when people don't recognize how important this matter is. Don't they see all the blessings they are forfeiting? Aren't they hungry to experience God's supernatural miracles and provision?

The pilgrims who trod the road to Jerusalem to celebrate God's feasts were *expectant.* As they sang the Psalms of Ascent, they felt their faith rise as they anticipated their appointment with Almighty God.

Remember: Each of the feasts is a personal invitation for you to enter into more of *God's presence.* This fact is one of the keys to understanding why they provide such a powerful way to receive breakthroughs in your life.

Jesus said the problems in your life are like "mountains" that you can speak to in faith and move out of your way (Matthew 17:20). While it's awesome that you've been given that kind of power and authority in the name of Jesus, Psalm 97:5 describes another way the troubles in your life can be remedied:

"The mountains melt like wax at the presence of the Lord!"

If your mountain refuses to move right away when you speak to it, you can use a different tactic — melting away your troubles by entering into the presence of the Lord. In God's awesome presence, sickness is healed…depression is lifted…addictions are overcome…poverty is defeated…and broken relationships are restored. With one touch from God, your problems can melt like candle wax!

Whether we realize it or not, every one of us is crying out for more of God's presence. Something inside us yearns to know Him, to experience intimacy with Him, and to offer the only thing we truly have to give Him…our worship.

That's really what the feasts are all about — an opportunity to draw closer to the Lord:

- **During Passover,** God deals with our sins and offers forgiveness and deliverance through the blood of the lamb.

- **During Pentecost,** we're invited to greater intimacy with the Lord through the power of the Holy Spirit.

- **During Tabernacles,** we're called upon to remember God's past faithfulness and then "tabernacle" with Him, free from the distractions of ordinary life.

My own journey into intimacy with the Lord began many years ago with a growing cry in my heart for a deeper relationship with Him. While reading Philippians 3, I came across these words by the apostle Paul: *"…that I may **know Him** and the power of His resurrection"* (v. 10).

I was blown away, thinking, "Paul, how could you possibly say this? You wrote two-thirds of the New Testament, and *you're* talking about wanting to know the Lord better? If you felt like you didn't know God

well enough, what about the rest of us?"

Then the realization dawned that we're all on a journey into the heart of God, and none of us is yet at the deep place of intimacy where He desires us to be. Paul recognized he wasn't yet where God was calling him to be, but he was pressing upward toward God's call to intimacy.

Desperately hungry to know God like this, I prayed, "Lord, I truly want to know You. I don't want to just know *about* You...I want to *know You.*"

I then heard the Lord speak to my spirit: *"David, do you want to go to that next level with Me...beyond acquaintance, beyond friendship, and beyond just knowing about Me? Are you really longing for a deeper relationship?"*

I responded, "Yes, Lord, I truly want an intimate relationship with You."

At this, He replied, *"David, if you really want to get to know Me, why aren't you spending more time with Me?"*

When God asked me this, it hurt. It hurt a lot. I *did* spend time with the Lord, but He was gently and firmly convicting me that I usually allowed my overcrowded schedule to limit my time with Him.

To make sure I got the point, He continued, *"If you truly want to know Me, you're going to need to spend more time with Me."*

I thought about this for a while. There are lots of ways we can get to know someone. Often when we meet a person for the first time, we've already heard *about* them, but we don't really *know* them. The only way we get to know someone is by spending TIME with them. That's exactly what the Lord was asking of me, and I believe it's a crucial message for you as well.

During the feasts, you and I have an appointment to come away from the hustle and bustle of life and spend time with our Heavenly Father. Not only will we experience *"fullness of joy"* in His presence (Psalm 16:11), but we will also be amazed by how quickly our troubles begin to melt away.

26 A FORMULA TO DEFEAT THE DEVIL

The Bible makes it clear that Satan is real. He once stood in the presence of God. He even led worship in Heaven before God's throne.

But Satan sinned. The Bible also says a rebellion occurred in Heaven, and a vast army of angels chose to rebel with Satan against their God and Creator. Some theologians point to Revelation 12:4 and suggest that a third of the angels followed Satan and rebelled against God. Whether it was a third of the angels or not isn't important. The critical fact is that there's now a vast army of fallen angels, and their master is Satan.

Satan goes by many names in the Bible. In Revelation 12:9 he's called *"the great dragon…that serpent of old."* In other places he's called the devil, Lucifer, and Satan. John 8:44 calls him the Evil One. Each of these names reveals a different aspect of Satan's diabolical personality.

Describing the devil as *"the accuser"* thrown down to earth in the Last Days, Revelation 12:10-11 provides a surefire strategy for victory over him:

> *They overcame him by the blood of the Lamb and by the word of their testimony, and they did not love their lives to the death.*

Originally foreshadowed in the Feast of Passover, Jesus' blood is a crucial weapon in your arsenal against Satan. It's the seal of your

salvation…the proof of your forgiveness…and the sign of your covenant relationship with Almighty God! The devil's accusations are nullified whenever you apply the blood of Jesus to your spiritual warfare.

The blood referred to in Revelation 12:11 as "*the blood of the* **Lamb**" is the blood of Jesus, *"the Lamb of God who takes away the sin of the world"* (John 1:29). In the Feast of Passover, His shed blood was beautifully depicted hundreds of years before He was even born:

> *Then the whole assembly of the congregation of Israel shall kill [the Passover lamb] at twilight. And they shall take some of the blood and put it on the two doorposts and on the lintel of the houses where they eat it…*

> *For I will pass through the land of Egypt on that night, and will strike all the firstborn in the land of Egypt, both man and beast; and against all the gods of Egypt I will execute judgment: I am the LORD. Now the blood shall be a sign for you on the houses where you are.* ***And when I see the blood, I will pass over you; and the plague shall not be on you to destroy you when I strike the land of Egypt*** (Exodus 12:6-7, 12-13).

Do you see the supernatural protection you have when you choose to apply the blood of Jesus to the doorposts of your heart…your mind…your body…your family…your finances…and every other aspect of your life?

- When the thief comes to steal, kill, and destroy…

- When the devil comes as a roaring lion, seeking someone to devour…

- When demons of sickness, poverty, lust, addiction, fear, or depression look for someone to prey upon…

They will have to go past you and find someone else to attack!

Although preaching on "the power of the blood" isn't very fashionable these days, the Bible says *"without shedding of blood there is no forgiveness"* (Hebrews 9:22). This theme has been described as a "scarlet thread" that extends throughout the entire Bible, from Genesis to Revelation.

It's interesting that Rahab the harlot was saved by tying a *"cord of scarlet thread"* to the window of her house (Joshua 2:17-21). While everyone else in Jericho was killed in battle, she and her family were kept safe by the scarlet cord! Similar to the Passover blood on a family's doorposts, this cord represents the protection you have from evil because of the blood of our Passover Lamb, Jesus.

Rahab's salvation wasn't based on her own virtue or righteousness — she was a *prostitute!* Her only hope for safety was the scarlet cord that kept her safe from attack.

I encourage you to take a few minutes to pause and pray. As the Feast of Passover so powerfully depicts, you need to make sure "the blood of the Lamb" has been applied to every area of your life. Be certain you aren't basing your relationship with God on your own goodness but on the "scarlet cord" that testifies of Jesus' death on your behalf.

Remember: Before the devil will flee from you, you first must submit yourself fully to God (James 4:7). But then you can claim the powerful truth of Revelation 12:11 over your life by declaring: "I am overcoming Satan by the blood of the Lamb, by the word of my testimony, and because I will not love my own life, even when faced with death!"

The Lord hasn't planned any defeats for you, my friend. He has given you *"the blood of the Lamb"* and other powerful spiritual weapons to defeat the enemy. Each of God's *"appointed times"* is a VICTORY celebration, and the Bible tells us to expect a triumphant life in Christ:

Thanks be to God, who always leads us in triumph in Christ, and manifests through us the sweet aroma of the knowledge of Him in every place (2 Corinthians 2:14).

This victorious life is God's will for YOU! Draw near to Him today. Learn to use the powerful weapons He's given you to defeat the enemy and enter into a life of abundance (John 10:10).

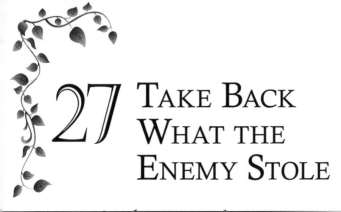

27 TAKE BACK WHAT THE ENEMY STOLE

When I share with people how they can live in victory, I'm often asked a very important question. "David," they ask me, "although it's great to know I can experience victory today, what about all the things I've already lost along the way? Is it too late to take back what the enemy has stolen from me?"

That's a great question, isn't it? Perhaps you've been asking yourself the same thing, wondering if there's any way to recover what the devil has stolen from you. Maybe you've been attacked in your family, your health, your finances, or your peace of mind—and you surely could use a miracle from God to recover your losses.

Well, I have good news! Even though the thief may have robbed you (John 10:10), God wants to restore whatever has been stolen. The Bible is full of stories about people who were empowered to take back what the enemy had stolen—and the Feast of Passover is a great example of this.

Remember, the first Passover was instituted by God when the Israelites had been in slavery in Egypt for 430 years. That's a long time! For generation after generation, God's people had suffered cruel oppression—but all that was about to change, in quite dramatic fashion.

The people of Israel did as Moses had instructed; they asked the

*Egyptians for clothing and articles of silver and gold. The LORD caused the Egyptians to **look favorably** on the Israelites, and they gave the Israelites whatever they asked for. So they stripped the Egyptians of their wealth!* (Exodus 12:35-36 NLT).

What an amazing turnaround. For hundreds of years, the Egyptians had been their cruel captors, and now the Israelites were asking not just for *freedom,* but for *reparations* as well. Remarkably, *God's favor* brought about favor even from the *enemies* of His people.

The Israelites had been robbed of their blessings for centuries, but now they left their captivity with unimaginable riches and prosperity. Instead of being paupers and beggars, they were abundantly blessed with silver, gold, clothing, and livestock (vs. 35-38).

Friend, this is a powerful illustration of God's desire to turnaround *your* negative circumstances and bless you beyond your wildest dreams. Even if you have been in some kind of spiritual, financial, or relational captivity for a long time, your breakthrough can come with stunning speed.

Remember: God has appointments to bless you through His *"appointed times."* When you follow His instructions, you can confidently expect to take back what the enemy has stolen from you.

As you set your heart to obey the Lord and believe His promises, I encourage you to meditate on these great Biblical examples of people who "plundered" the enemy and recovered *everything* that had been stolen:

- Abraham recovered *everything* the enemy stole from Lot (Genesis 14:16).

- David recovered *everything* the enemy stole from Ziklag (1 Samuel 30:18-19).

- God's law says a thief must pay back even *more* than what he stole (Exodus 22:1, 7).

- Job was blessed with *double* of everything Satan had stolen from him (Job 42:10).

- In the book of Joel, God promised to restore even *years* of the enemy's plunder (Joel 2:24-26).

If the devil has stolen something from you, don't assume it's gone forever. Take a moment and recommit your life fully to the Lord. Ask Him to give you His perspective and His strategies for overcoming the enemy's attacks. Take Him at His Word that He will reverse your losses and bless you with His presence, power, and provision!

RECEIVE THE POWER TO PROSPER 28

The book of Deuteronomy is Moses' summary of God's instructions to the Israelites during their sojourn through the wilderness, from Egypt to the brink of the Promised Land. In chapter eight, Moses reviewed some of the lessons God had given them and some of the promises He had made if they would obey Him:

> *Every commandment which I command you today you must be careful to observe, that you may live and multiply, and go in and possess the land of which the LORD swore to your fathers* (v. 1).

My friend, these words form a vital foundation for what the Lord wants to do in YOUR life today. Just like the Israelites, perhaps you are standing on the brink of some important decision or new beginning. Although you're close enough to see your Promised Land, there still are some important steps of faith needed if you're going to cross the Jordan River and *"go in and possess the land"* God has promised you.

God says He wants you to *"live and multiply,"* and *The Message* renders this *"live and prosper"* (v. 1). This abundant life becomes possible when you are *"careful to observe"* God's commandments. Instead of focusing on your earthly needs (*"bread alone"*), you learn to live *"by every word that proceeds from the mouth of the LORD"* (v. 3).

When the Israelites obeyed the Lord, they saw His faithfulness in

miraculous ways: *"Your garments did not wear out on you, nor did your foot swell these forty years"* (v. 4). Imagine that: having clothes that lasted you 40 years, and walking in continual good health despite an arduous journey through the desert.

But God told the Israelites that the BEST was still to come if they would "walk in His ways and to fear Him":

> *The LORD your God is bringing you into a **good land**, a land of brooks of water, of fountains and springs, that flow out of valleys and hills; a land of wheat and barley, of vines and fig trees and pomegranates, a land of olive oil and honey; a land in which you will eat bread **without scarcity,** in which you **will lack nothing**... When you have eaten and are full, then you shall bless the LORD your God for the good land which He has given you* (vs. 6-10).

The feasts of the Lord are designed to point you toward God's faithful love and provision, my friend. Your Heavenly Father wants to bring you into *"a good land"* where you will live *"without scarcity"* and *"lack nothing."* What an awesome God!

This chapter goes on to present a warning to the Israelites not to forget the Lord once they had been brought into the land of MORE THAN ENOUGH. They're reminded of how God had brought them *"from the house of bondage"* (during Passover), given them His Law (during Pentecost), and provided for them in the wilderness (commemorated during the Feast of Tabernacles). Notice that the feasts serve as a reminder of what God has done in the past, an affirmation of His presence with you today, and a prophetic signpost of what He is planning for your future.

Just as Deuteronomy 8 was meant to prepare the Israelites for the incredible land of incredible abundance God was bringing them into, this is also a message of encouragement to you, my friend. When you

finally step into the land of MORE THAN ENOUGH, don't say in your heart, *"My power and the might of my hand have gained me this wealth"* (v. 17). Instead, remember and give thanks to the Lord, *"for it is He who gives you* **power to get wealth,** *that He may establish His* **covenant** *which He swore to your fathers, as it is this day"* (v. 18).

Let those words sink into your heart. God is giving you the power to *"get wealth"* as you walk in a covenant relationship with Him. The New Living Translation says God *"gives you power to be successful."*

Take a moment to thank the Lord for His faithfulness to you in the past. Praise Him for the *"good land"* He is getting ready to bring you into. Lay hold of His promise to empower you for prosperity and success.

29 CLAIM YOUR FULL INHERITANCE

When Jesus died for us on the cross, by far the greatest blessing was having our sins forgiven and being reconciled to God. Hundreds of years in advance, the prophet Isaiah had painted a stunning prophetic picture of the atoning work Jesus would accomplish for us by His shed blood:

> *He was wounded for our transgressions, He was bruised for our iniquities; the chastisement of our peace was upon Him; and with His stripes we are healed. All we like sheep have gone astray; we have turned every one to his own way; and the LORD has laid on Him the iniquity of us all* (Isaiah 53:5-6).

We're reminded of this fantastic truth whenever we celebrate the feasts of the Lord, especially Passover and the Day of Atonement. During Old Testament times, the high priest could only go into the Holy of Holies once a year, bringing the blood of an animal sacrifice with him on the Day of Atonement (Leviticus 16). However, at the very moment when Jesus died on the cross, Matthew 27:51 says, *"the veil of the temple was torn in two from top to bottom."*

The thick, heavy veil that hung from ceiling to floor in the temple had created a barrier to intimacy with God. But because the veil was torn in two, you now have full access to the presence of God through

the blood of Jesus. The book of Hebrews explains that Jesus Himself is now your *"merciful and faithful High Priest"* (Hebrews 2:17). And He doesn't have to offer endless sacrifices, because He has atoned for your sins *"once for all when He offered up Himself"* (Hebrews 7:27).

Friend, whatever sins and transgressions you have committed, you can know this: Jesus paid the penalty by His death on the cross. You are reconciled to God on the basis of faith, because Jesus has already purchased your atonement.

But often we as Believers are unaware of the full extent of our inheritance as God's blood-bought, covenant children. Isaiah's description of the atonement doesn't stop with a declaration of your forgiveness, but it says Jesus *also* purchased your peace, healing, and well-being.

Later in the chapter, Isaiah describes even *more* blessings that result from Jesus' sacrificial death on your behalf: blessings for your children, a prolonged life, and God's favor and prosperity (v. 10). What a great inheritance!

I encourage you to meditate on the amazing benefits Jesus purchased for you *"through the blood of the everlasting covenant"*:

> *Now may the God of peace who brought up our Lord Jesus from the dead, that great Shepherd of the sheep, through the blood of the everlasting covenant, make you complete in every good work to do His will, working in you what is well pleasing in His sight, through Jesus Christ, to whom be glory forever and ever. Amen* (Hebrews 13:20-21).

When you are walking in a covenant relationship with God, you experience Him as *"the God of peace"* no matter what difficult circumstances you may be facing. Jesus becomes your *"great Shepherd,"* and you are made *"complete in every good work to do His will."* All of this is so that you can be *"well pleasing in His sight."*

This covenant relationship with God has sometimes been called the Great Exchange or the Divine Exchange:

- Jesus took your sin upon Himself so that you could be *"the righteousness of God in Him"* (2 Corinthians 5:21).

- He took your sicknesses so that you could be healed (1 Peter 2:24).

- He took your curses so that you could receive His blessings (Galatians 3:13-14).

- He took your poverty so that you could experience His abundance (2 Corinthians 8:9, John 10:10).

- He bore your griefs and sorrows so you could receive His incredible peace (Isaiah 53:4-5).

- He tasted death so that you might have eternal life (Romans 6:23, Hebrews 2:9).

My friend, God's *"appointed times"* were instituted to remind you of the abounding blessings you've been given in Christ. Take a moment right now and give Him thanks for the amazing covenant He has made with you through the cross.

YOUR TABERNACLE WITH THE LORD 30

Of God's three *"appointed times,"* the Feast of Tabernacles is generally the one that Christians know the least about. Although many Believers haven't given much thought to the significance of Passover or Pentecost either, Tabernacles is *completely* off their radar screen.

In all likelihood, Jesus was born during the Feast of Tabernacles. It's pretty clear He wasn't born on December 25 — a day chosen simply because it coincided with the pagan holiday of Saturnalia, a weeklong celebration of lawlessness and immorality.

Although the Bible doesn't specify the date when our Savior was born, we are given some clues on the season of His birth. For example, John 1:14 literally reads, *"The Word [i.e., Jesus] became flesh, and tabernacled among us, and we saw His glory"* (John 1:14). The Greek word used here is *skēnoō,* which means to temporarily dwell in a tent or tabernacle. This is exactly what the Israelites were told to do during the Feast of Tabernacles, as they reenacted God's faithfulness to them during their sojourn through the wilderness.

Do you see what a beautiful picture this is? At the same time as God's people were living in their temporary shelters during the Feast of Tabernacles, their long-awaited Messiah came and tabernacled among them!

Throughout the Bible, you can see powerful word pictures of what it means to abide with the Lord in His tabernacle or sanctuary. One of my favorite passages is Psalm 91:1-16:

He who dwells in the secret place of the Most High
Shall abide under the shadow of the Almighty.
I will say of the LORD, "He is my refuge and my fortress;
My God, in Him I will trust."

Surely He shall deliver you from the snare of the fowler
And from the perilous pestilence.
He shall cover you with His feathers,
And under His wings you shall take refuge;
His truth shall be your shield and buckler.
You shall not be afraid of the terror by night,
Nor of the arrow that flies by day,
Nor of the pestilence that walks in darkness,
Nor of the destruction that lays waste at noonday.

A thousand may fall at your side,
And ten thousand at your right hand;
But it shall not come near you.
Only with your eyes shall you look,
And see the reward of the wicked.

Because you have made the LORD, who is my refuge,
Even the Most High, your dwelling place,
No evil shall befall you,
Nor shall any plague come near your dwelling;
For He shall give His angels charge over you,
To keep you in all your ways.
In their hands they shall bear you up,
Lest you dash your foot against a stone.
You shall tread upon the lion and the cobra,

The young lion and the serpent you shall trample underfoot.

"Because he has set his love upon Me, therefore I will deliver him;
I will set him on high, because he has known My name.
He shall call upon Me, and I will answer him;
I will be with him in trouble;
I will deliver him and honor him.
With long life I will satisfy him,
And show him My salvation."

My friend, I encourage to take time to read through this amazing psalm line by line, noticing God's promises to YOU when you tabernacle with Him in His *"secret place."* Protection from harm…deliverance from fear…honor and blessings…confidence and peace of mind… and a satisfying, long life — these are just a few of the many benefits of learning to abide in God's presence.

If you are feeling overwhelmed by the cares of life today, take time to meditate on King David's declaration about finding shelter and provision in the tabernacle of the Lord:

Hear my cry, O God;
Attend to my prayer.
From the end of the earth I will cry to You,
*When my heart is **overwhelmed;***
Lead me to the rock that is higher than I.
*For You have been a **shelter** for me,*
*A **strong tower** from the enemy.*
I will abide in Your tabernacle forever;
I will trust in the shelter of Your wings (Psalm 61:1-4).

Remember: God's *"appointed times"* — and especially the Feast of Tabernacles — provide you with a fantastic opportunity to experience the life-changing benefits of dwelling in the presence of the Lord. He will be your *"strong tower"* and shelter amid life's storms.

31 OBTAIN YOUR DOUBLE PORTION

As we've already seen, the feasts of Passover, Pentecost, and Tabernacles are special seasons on God's calendars—seasons of supernatural harvests. Each of these feasts reminds us that there are two different economies in which you can choose to live.

The world's economic system says work hard, be smart, and you'll be rewarded. It's all up to you. In contrast, God's economic system is based on the law of seedtime and harvest. He says He will take care of you if you're obedient to His commandments and faithful in your tithes and offerings.

While the world says to hold on to what you have, God says just the opposite: *"Give, and it will be given to you"* (Luke 6:38). And while the world says hoarding your wealth brings prosperity, God warns that withholding what you have will lead to poverty (Proverbs 11:24-25).

Every promise in the Word of God has a *condition* attached to it. We see this in Malachi 3:10, where the Lord says, *"Prove Me."* As He says in so many other scriptures, He tells us, "If *you'll* do 'this,' *I'll* do 'that.'" This is another stunning reminder that although the Lord's amazing love, grace, mercy, and forgiveness are 100% unconditional, His blessings are quite different: 100% conditional.

As I mentioned earlier, God promises in Exodus 23 and Leviticus 23

that if you bring your offerings and obey what He's told you to do, He will pour out seven specific covenant promises in your life:

1. An angel of God will be assigned to protect you and lead you to your miracles.

2. God will be an enemy to your enemies.

3. The Lord will prosper you.

4. God will take sickness away from you.

5. You will not die before your appointed time.

6. Increase and an inheritance will be yours.

7. What the enemy has stolen will be returned to you.

As wonderful as these blessings are, God amazingly offers you seven *additional* "double portion" blessings when you observe the Feast of Tabernacles. Tabernacles is a time to commemorate God's care and protection of His people when they journeyed from Egypt to the Promised Land. During the Feast of Tabernacles, we're reminded each year…

There is shelter, protection, and provision in the tabernacle of God's presence!

The Feast of Tabernacles is preceded by ten "Days of Awe" and then the Day of Atonement. These "high holy days" are 10 days of repentance, beginning when a shofar sounds on the Feast of Trumpets (*Rosh Hashanah*), calling people to a time of sober soul-searching.

Joel 2 reflects this same theme, calling God's people to repentance, fasting, and holiness: *"Blow a trumpet in Zion"* (v. 1)…*"Consecrate a fast, proclaim a solemn assembly, gather the people, sanctify the congregation"* (vs. 15-16).

This passage in Joel goes on to list seven special "double portion" blessings the Lord wants to provide for His people during the Feast of Tabernacles season:

1. **A double portion of rain.** *"He will cause the rain to come down for you — the **former** rain, **AND** the **latter** rain in the first month"* (v. 23). Although the periods of the former and latter rains were usually separated by many months, God wants to give you a ***double*** blessing during the Feast of Tabernacles season so you can receive *both* of these outpourings of provision *"in the first month."* This double portion was of great practical necessity to the Israelites, because the harvest blessings of the Feast of Tabernacles season had to last them a longer period than the interval between Passover and Pentecost (just 50 days) or between Pentecost and Tabernacles (about four months).

2. **Financial prosperity.** *" The threshing floors shall be full of wheat, and the vats shall overflow with new wine and oil"* (v. 24).

3. **Restoration.** *"I will restore to you the years that the swarming locust has eaten"* (v. 25).

4. **Special miracles.** *"You shall...praise the name of the Lord your God, who has dealt wondrously with you"* (v. 26)...*"and I will show wonders"* (v. 30).

5. **God's presence and favor.** *"You shall know that I am in the midst of Israel...My people shall never be put to shame"* (v. 27).

6. **Blessings for your sons and daughters.** *"Your sons and your daughters shall prophesy...your young men shall see visions"* (v. 28).

7. **Deliverance from harm or oppression.** *"Whoever calls on the name of the Lord will be delivered"* (v. 32).

In order to unlock this remarkable "double portion" of God's blessings, it's crucial that you fulfill His *conditions* and not appear before Him *"empty-handed"* (Deuteronomy 16:16). At these special times each year, the Israelites were to present their offerings to the Lord from the seeds they had sown and the harvests He had given them—and the same principle holds true for you to today.

Do you want to reap God's BEST? Do you want to see Him move in your life as never before? Then begin now to prepare your heart and your special offering to the Lord. I'm convinced that if you need a miracle breakthrough in your body…your relationship with the Lord… your marriage…your children…your emotions…or your finances…

The Feast of Tabernacles
is your opportunity to obey God and receive
His DOUBLE PORTION blessings!

32 GET TWICE AS MUCH

There's a special reason *why* the Feast of Tabernacles is associated with "double portion" blessings for God's people. The Feast of Tabernacles is the third event on God's *"appointed times"* calendar, along with the Feast of Passover and Feast of Pentecost. However, it is actually one of SEVEN feasts listed in Leviticus 23:

1. **Passover**
2. **Unleavened Bread**
3. **Firstfruits**
4. **Pentecost (the Feast of Weeks)**
5. **Trumpets**
6. **The Day of Atonement**
7. **Tabernacles**

The fact that Tabernacles is the seventh feast has profound significance, especially in light of this introductory statement in Leviticus 23:2-3:

> *The feasts of the LORD, which you shall proclaim to be holy convocations, these are My feasts. Six days shall work be done, but the seventh day is a Sabbath of solemn rest, a holy convocation. You shall do no work on it; it is the Sabbath of the LORD in all your dwellings.*

Just as the *seventh-day* Sabbath was set apart by God as a time of rest, the *seventh feast* follows that same pattern. And the Israelites knew that something very important occurred prior to every Sabbath as they journeyed through the wilderness. God told them in Exodus 16:

> *Behold, I will rain bread from heaven for you. And the people shall go out and gather a certain quota every day, that I may test them, whether they will walk in My law or not. And it shall be on the* **sixth day** *that they shall prepare what they bring in, and* **it shall be twice as much as they gather daily** (vs. 4-5).

> *So they gathered it every morning, every man according to his need. And when the sun became hot, it melted.*

> *And so it was, on the sixth day, that they gathered* **twice as much bread,** *two omers for each one. And all the rulers of the congregation came and told Moses. Then he said to them, "This is what the LORD has said: 'Tomorrow is a Sabbath rest, a holy Sabbath to the LORD. Bake what you will bake today, and boil what you will boil; and lay up for yourselves all that remains, to be kept until morning'"* (vs. 21-23).

> *See! For the LORD has given you the Sabbath; therefore He gives you on the sixth day* **bread for two days.** *Let every man remain in his place; let no man go out of his place on the seventh day. So the people rested on the seventh day* (vs. 29-30).

You see, because work was prohibited on the seventh day, the Israelites had to collect a **double portion** of manna on the day before the Sabbath. And that same principle holds true when you celebrate the *seventh feast,* the Feast of Tabernacles. Since it is instituted by God as a time of rest and rejuvenation, He offers to provide you with *twice as much provision* as you ordinarily would receive!

But also notice that the Israelites were unable to "hoard" their

manna. They had to receive it in God's appointed way, flowing in His perfect schedule. And if they *failed* to receive their double portion when it was offered, they would suffer lack on their day of rest.

Don't miss out on your double portion, my friend. God is offering you *twice as much provision* at his *"appointed time."*

ENTER INTO GOD'S REST 33

I meet so many people today who are overwhelmed with the cares of life. Frazzled by the hustle and bustle of their daily obligations, they find themselves completely exhausted and discouraged.

If you are feeling this way today, I have good news! If you need *"times of refreshing"* from the cares of life, Acts 3:19 tells you exactly where that may be found: in *"the presence of the Lord."*

The Feast of Tabernacles is designed by the Lord as a time for you to find rest and be refreshed in His presence.

The fact that Tabernacles is the *seventh* annual feast has profound significance, especially in light of this introductory statement in God's description of *"My feasts"* in Leviticus 23:2-3:

> *The feasts of the LORD, which you shall proclaim to be holy convocations, these are My feasts. Six days shall work be done, but the seventh day is a Sabbath of solemn rest, a holy convocation. You shall do no work on it; it is the Sabbath of the LORD in all your dwellings.*

Before describing the seven feasts His people are to celebrate, it's significant that the Lord reminds us here of the *Sabbath* principle: There should be six days of work, followed by a day of *"solemn rest"* when we

do no work at all. This was an important pattern originally set by God at the beginning of His creation (Genesis 2:1-3) and then reaffirmed when the Law was given to Moses on Mount Sinai (Exodus 20:8-11).

As the seventh feast, Tabernacles becomes linked to the principle of the Sabbath. God's "work" has already been completed during the other six feasts, and now it is time to rejoice and enter into His rest! A double portion of manna has already been gathered, so there's no more work to do during this time of rest and celebration.

My friend, Jesus extends this beautiful invitation to you in Matthew 11:28-30:

> *Come to Me, all you who labor and are heavy laden, and I will give you rest. Take My yoke upon you and learn from Me, for I am gentle and lowly in heart, and you will find rest for your souls. For My yoke is easy and My burden is light.*

Tabernacles is a wonderful opportunity each year to enter into God's rest. The author of the book of Hebrews tells us:

> *There remains therefore a rest for the people of God. For he who has entered His rest has himself also ceased from his works as God did from His.*
>
> *Let us therefore be diligent to enter that rest, lest anyone fall according to the same example of disobedience* (Hebrews 4:9-11).

Don't let unbelief or disobedience keep you from entering God's rest! It's a precious gift to you from your Heavenly Father — beautifully depicted in the seventh feast, the Feast of Tabernacles. Exodus 20:11 tells us, *"The LORD **BLESSED** the Sabbath day and hallowed it,"* and the same is true about how He has blessed the Feast of Tabernacles. As the seventh feast, it is set apart as a special time of blessing and refreshing.

Do you want to find this amazing *"rest for your soul"*? Then the Bible

says you need to return to the *"ancient paths,"* my friend:

> *Stand at the crossroads and look;*
> *ask for the **ancient paths,***
> *ask where the good way is, and walk in it,*
> *and you will find **rest for your souls*** (Jeremiah 6:16 NIV).

When you incline your heart to the Lord and walk in His ways, He will give you rest and demonstrate His faithfulness:

> *Blessed be the LORD, who has **given rest to His people** Israel,*
> *according to all that He promised. There has not failed one word*
> *of all His good promise, which He promised through His servant*
> *Moses. May the LORD our God be with us, as He was with our*
> *fathers. May He not leave us nor forsake us, that He may incline*
> *our hearts to Himself, to walk in all His ways, and to keep His*
> *commandments and His statutes and His judgments, which He*
> *commanded our fathers* (1 Kings 8:56-58).

Remember: God's *"appointed times"* are part of the *"ancient paths"* He has prepared for you. They are times of blessing, refreshing, and peace. Give Him your best, follow His instructions, and get ready to experience amazing, deep rest for your soul.

34 RIVERS OF LIVING WATER

Are you thirsty for more of the Lord today? This was a recurring theme in the Psalms:

> *As the deer pants for the water brooks,*
> *So pants my soul for You, O God.*
> *My soul thirsts for God, for the living God.*
> *When shall I come and appear before God?* (Psalm 42:1-2)

> *O God, You are my God;*
> *Early will I seek You;*
> *My soul thirsts for You;*
> *My flesh longs for You*
> *In a dry and thirsty land*
> *Where there is no water.*
> *So I have looked for You in the sanctuary,*
> *To see Your power and Your glory.*

> *Because Your lovingkindness is better than life,*
> *My lips shall praise You.*
> *Thus I will bless You while I live;*
> *I will lift up my hands in Your name.*
> *My soul shall be satisfied as with marrow and fatness,*
> *And my mouth shall praise You with joyful lips* (Psalm 63:1-5).

These passages speak of the psalmist's desperate thirst for the Lord and His presence. He speaks of *taking action* to quench this thirst — panting…appearing before God…seeking God early in the morning… looking for the Lord in His sanctuary…beholding His power and glory…and praising Him with uplifted hands.

As a result, the psalmist comes to this beautiful conclusion: *"My soul shall be satisfied…"* This is God's will for YOU as well, my friend. He wants to satisfy your soul and quench your thirst as you seek Him — even in *"a dry and thirsty land."*

But perhaps you didn't realize the Feast of Tabernacles presents an opportunity to drink deeply of God's refreshing, satisfying waters. On the seventh and final day of the Feast of Tabernacles each year, the climax came when the priest poured out water in the temple. This ceremony was a petition to God to send rain for the coming year's crops.

However, one year when Jesus was celebrating the Feast of Tabernacles, He interrupted this religious ritual with a stunning claim:

> *If anyone thirsts, let him come to Me and drink. He who believes in Me, as the Scripture has said, out of his heart will flow rivers of living water* (John 7:37-38).

This no doubt was quite upsetting to the religious leaders. Jesus was offering to quench people's spiritual thirst, not by religious rituals, but by inviting them to come to HIM and drink.

My friend, if you are still thirsty after all your efforts to find fulfillment, why not heed Jesus' invitation to come to Him and drink? Not only will your own thirst be satisfied, but *"rivers of living water"* will flow out from you to bless others.

Remember: Jesus made this incredible offer during the Feast of

Tabernacles. Of course, He wants you to come to Him today and *every* day. But God instituted His *"appointed times"* as special opportunities to be blessed and refreshed. These are appointments you don't want to miss!

FACING THE CROSSROADS 35

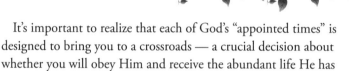

It's important to realize that each of God's "appointed times" is designed to bring you to a crossroads — a crucial decision about whether you will obey Him and receive the abundant life He has promised.

- *At Passover,* you must choose to receive His forgiveness and deliverance from the bondage of sin and Satan.

- *At Pentecost,* you must choose to submit to His will and be empowered by His Spirit.

- *At Tabernacles,* you must stop your other activities to "tabernacle" with the Lord and rejoice in His faithfulness.

Notice that these were *annual feasts,* sending a message from God that you should continually reaffirm your decision to wholeheartedly follow Him. When the Israelites faithfully observed God's three "*appointed times,*" they had *regular* opportunities to renew their covenant with the Lord.

God will never be satisfied with a half-hearted, compromised commitment, my friend. We see this at the end of Joshua's life, when he challenged the Israelites to make a firm, deliberate, personal choice for themselves and their families:

Choose for yourselves this day whom you will serve, whether the gods which your fathers served that were on the other side of the River, or the gods of the Amorites, in whose land you dwell. But as for me and my house, we will serve the LORD
(Joshua 24:15).

Take a few moments to look at your life today, asking yourself how Joshua's challenging words would apply. Have you truly chosen to follow the Lord with all your heart? Or are you just going through the motions?

It's not surprising that this matter of choice was such a touchy issue with Joshua. Throughout his life, he had witnessed painful examples of people making wrong choices. One of the worst cases was when the Israelites allowed fear and unbelief to keep them out of the Promised Land—resulting in 40 years of wandering in the wilderness (Numbers 13:1-14:24). Joshua became keenly aware of how serious our choices are, for these decisions determine our consequences…our rewards… and our destiny.

Joshua's exhortation for people to "choose" whom they would serve was an echo of God's earlier challenge in Deuteronomy 30:15-20:

See, I have set before you today life and prosperity, and death and adversity; in that I command you today to love the LORD your God, to walk in His ways and to keep His commandments and His statutes and His judgments, that you may live and multiply, and that the LORD your God may bless you in the land where you are entering to possess it. But if your heart turns away and you will not obey, but are drawn away and worship other gods and serve them, I declare to you today that you shall surely perish. You will not prolong your days in the land where you are crossing the Jordan to enter and possess it.

I call heaven and earth to witness against you today, that I have

*set before you life and death, the blessing and the curse. So **choose life** in order that you may live, you and your descendants, by loving the LORD your God, by obeying His voice, and by holding fast to Him; for this is your life and the length of your days, that you may live in the land which the LORD swore to your fathers, to Abraham, Isaac, and Jacob, to give them.*

Please take time to read these words and let them sink in. God offers you a sobering choice—a choice that will affect your destiny. You can experience life or death…the blessing or the curse. And in case you aren't quite sure which choice to make, God makes it absolutely clear: *"CHOOSE LIFE!"*

You see, God's blessings aren't automatic, but must be actively and aggressively chosen. If you haven't made a clear decision to obey the Lord, then you've chosen the curse instead of the blessing. There's no neutral ground!

God wants to bless you, and the devil wants to destroy you — so the choice is *yours!* If you still don't believe me, take a look at Deuteronomy 28, an entire chapter dedicated to listing the blessings of obedience and the curses for disobedience.

God put these admonitions in His Word because He wants to bless you! And He instituted the feasts of Passover, Pentecost, and Tabernacles for that same reason — to bless you in extraordinary ways. Each time you observe one of these *"appointed times"* on God's calendar, you are making a decision to enter into His best for your life.

36 YOUR NEW SEASON OF BLESSINGS

I've never been more convinced that God's heart is to give His people breakthroughs of supernatural blessings and abundance. As the apostles pointed out when they preached in Lystra, *"He did good and gave you rains from heaven and **fruitful seasons,** satisfying your hearts with food and gladness"* (Acts 14:17 NASB).

Take a moment to let that phrase sink in, my friend: *"fruitful seasons."* Does that sound like something you could use today? Something your weary heart longs for?

Like me, you've no doubt seen news reports of the world's struggling economy, but it's time to shake off the doom and gloom and get a new perspective. When you celebrate the feasts of the Lord and engage in His law of sowing and reaping, you can be sure of this:

God can bless you *despite* the struggling economy!

The Bible gives this amazing promise to those who obey Him:

> *The LORD will open to you **His good treasure,** the heavens, to give the rain to your land in its season, and **to bless ALL the work of your hand*** (Deuteronomy 28:12).

"But David," you may protest, "this hasn't been my experience. We're living in tough times, and I've really struggled the past few years."

If you're struggling, I understand. Barbara and I know what it's like to face challenges in our finances, health, relationships, and emotions. But we've learned that God is faithful, and we're praying for you to receive the breakthrough of blessings you need from Him.

Remember: Even many of the Bible's greatest heroes sometimes experienced times of testing or famine. Yet the Scriptures provide this incredible word of encouragement: *"In the days of famine they will have abundance"* (Psalm 37:19 NASB).

How is this supernatural abundance possible? Let me share two powerful Scriptural principles for how you can enter into God's season of blessings, even in difficult economic times…

1. You can't buy a blessing, but you CAN sow your way out of a problem.

In Genesis 26, Isaac faced *"a famine in the land"* (v. 1). This truly was a difficult problem, so what did he do? Instead of becoming miserly and hoarding his resources, he determined to *Sow more Seeds!*

> *Then Isaac **sowed** in that land, and **reaped** in the same year a **hundredfold**; and **the LORD blessed him**. The man **began to prosper**, and **continued prospering** until he **became very prosperous**; for he had possessions of flocks and possessions of herds and a great number of servants. So **the Philistines envied him*** (vs. 12-14).

Friend, as God did for Isaac, He wants to bless you with a miraculous harvest of blessings…the envy of those around you! Whether you need a financial breakthrough, a healing in your body, or the restoration of your relationship with a loved one, you can trust God by sowing *SEEDS* to meet your *NEEDS!*

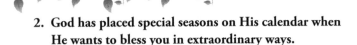

2. God has placed special seasons on His calendar when He wants to bless you in extraordinary ways.

Although God is *always* blessed when you act in faith to sow financial seeds into His Kingdom, the Bible says there are *"appointed times"* when He wants you to bring Him *special* offerings, so He can bless you with *extraordinary* miracles.

Barbara and I received this great testimony from an Inspiration Partner named Crystal, who sowed special offerings during the Lord's feasts:

> *"Although I've always given tithes and offerings to the Lord, He began answering my prayers in amazing ways when I started sowing special financial seeds during His 'appointed time' feasts of Passover, Pentecost, and Tabernacles. He helped me pay off all my bills, and now I'm debt-free! Plus, He enabled me to buy an apartment building. I only had asked to be able to buy a home of my own, but God gave me an entire apartment building, large enough for me and other family members! Thank you for teaching me about these critical seasons for God's blessings and breakthroughs."*

My friend, I'm convinced this can be *YOUR* season of God's favor too! It's His will that you walk in health…receive His abundance… and recover everything the devil has stolen from you! His Word clearly teaches that you WILL experience His miraculous provision when you obey Him, understand His seasons of blessing, and step out in faith to sow your seeds into His Kingdom.

Whatever turnaround you need in your life, your special season of blessings can start TODAY!

We are Here for You!

Helping to Change Your World Through Prayer

Do you need someone to pray with you about a financial need...a physical healing...an addiction...a broken relationship...or your spiritual growth with the Lord?

Our prayer ministers at the Inspiration Prayer Center are here for you. Because of God's goodness and faithfulness, His ears are attentive to the prayers made in this place (2 Chronicles 6:40).

"God does tremendous things as we pray for our Inspiration Partners over the phone. It's such a joy to see people reaching out to touch the Lord through prayer, and in return, to see God embrace them and meet their needs." – TERESA, Prayer Minister

Every day, Souls are being saved, miracles are taking place, and people are being impacted for God's eternal Kingdom! We continually receive amazing testimonies like these from people whose lives have been touched by our faithful prayer ministers:

Debt cancelled... *"After you prayed with me, I received the cancellation of a $23,000 medical bill. The hospital called it an act of charity, but I say it was God!"*
– MELVIN, New York

Son found... *"I had not heard from my son for five years, but I miraculously found him just two weeks after your prayer minister called!"* – Z.C., Missouri

Cancer gone... *"Thank you for standing with me in prayer and agreeing with me for my healing. The Lord has healed me of breast cancer!"* – NORMA, Michigan

Family restored... *"Thanks so much for your prayers. I've got my family back! The Lord gave me a great job, my wife was willing to take me back, and I've been clean from drugs and alcohol for almost a year. God is so good to us!"* – L.B., Colorado

This could be YOUR day for a miracle! Let our anointed ministry staff intercede with God on your behalf, praying the Prayer of Agreement for the breakthrough you need.

Resources to Help you
RELEASE GOD'S FAVOR
in Your Life

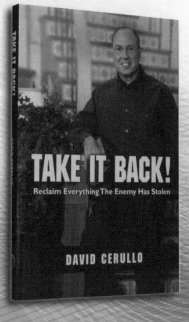

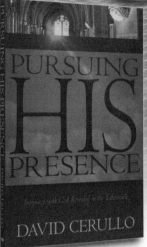

Visit **inspiration.org/gifts** or call one of the numbers below
to Sow a Seed for Souls and receive one or more of our life-changing
ministry resources to help release more of God's amazing favor in your life!

United States:
+1 803-578-1899

United Kingdom:
0845 683 0580

International:
+800 9982 4677

Caribbean:
877-487-7782

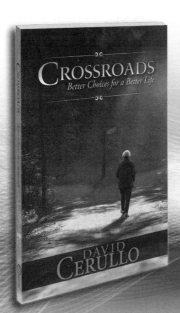